P9-CSA-961

Pocket Stones

Pocket Stones

A Child's Story of World War II
in the Philippines

For Evanston's children from Barbara-Ann Lewis

Barbara - Ann Gamboa Lewis
illustrated by
Barbara Pollak

Copyright © 2000 by Barbara-Ann Gamboa Lewis.

Library of Congress Number:		00-193164
ISBN #:	Hardcover	0-7388-5342-9
	Softcover	0-7388-5343-7

All rights reserved. No part of this book may be reproduced or transmitted in any form or by any means, electronic or mechanical, including photocopying, recording, or by any information storage and retrieval system, without permission in writing from the copyright owner.

This book was printed in the United States of America.

To order additional copies of this book, contact:
Xlibris Corporation
1-888-7-XLIBRIS
www.Xlibris.com
Orders@Xlibris.com

Contents

ACKNOWLEDGEMENTS 9

PREFACE 11

1 13

    Finding a Name

2 19

    Chickens and Children

3 25

    Open City

4 31

    The Rabbit That Wasn't

5 37

    A Room of My Own

6 45

    Guarding the Clothes

7 51

    My Father's Bad Temper

8 57

    Miss Behenna

9 63

    The Sad Japanese Officer

10 67

    The Spy

11 73

    Alcohol and Tobacco

12 79

    Loka and Loko

13 85

    Manila is Burning

14 91

    Hello Joe! Chocolate, Joe!

15 101

    Cherry Pie

16 107

    Lieutenant George Intile

17 117

    The Psychopathic Hospital

18 121

    Heroes on the Front Porch

19 129

    School Days

20 139

    Bad Times

21 149

    The Philippine General Hospital

22 155

    My Vacations

23 159

    The Sea, At Last

ADDENDA   165

WHAT HAPPENED TO EVERYBODY? 167

FELIPE AND DOREEN 171

SOMETHING ABOUT THE PHILIPPINES 179

To Dr. Richard B. Eisenstein
who uncovered the embers of my childhood,

and

to Snuffy and Trotsky
who were so much a part of it.

Acknowledgements

The author acknowledges the contributions of the following: Dimis Wyman who edited the manuscript; Gillian Virata who checked for accuracy regarding Philippine history; Mrs. Rosemary Phillip who provided some details of Doreen's younger years; Marya Hirsch who searched out ownership of song lyrics; Jimmie Davis and David Jacome of Peermusic for granting gratis permission to use the lyrics of the song "You Are My Sunshine"; Steven van Leeuwen, publisher, Bartleby.com for gratis permission to use the poem "Sea-Fever" by John Masefield, from Untermeyer, Louis. Modern British Poetry. New York, Harcourt, Brace and Howe, 1920, Bartleby.com, 1999. Margaret Raymo of Houghton-Miflin who kindly made comments on the original manuscript; the staff of Xlibris for their help during final book production. The excerpt from "My Last Farewell" by Dr. Jose Rizal was taken from "The Pride of the Malay Race" by Dr. Rafael Palma and Roman Ozaeta, Prentice Hall, 1949.

Preface

This is a true story about childhood during the years of World War II in the Philippines. It is a story about real people whose names have not been changed. If I offend anyone, it is not intentional but simply the truth as I remember it. Addenda to the story provide other information that may be of interest to some readers.

This book is written for my grandchildren and for all children who are eight to twelve years old. World War II was a long time ago, and the Philippines is a far-away place for children in other parts of the world, but I hope readers everywhere will discover in this story that some things are the same for all children, whenever the time, wherever the place.

B.G. Lewis
Evanston, Illinois
November 2000

I knew what I was looking for – a name that meant pirates and ships, sails roaring across the stormy oceans.

1

Finding a Name

"What's my name, Mommy?" I, Pooh, was ten years old and curious.

"You know what your name is." My mother's face was beautiful, but it was thin and there was a little frown on her forehead as she looked at me.

"No, I mean my REAL name, not my nickname."

"You don't have a real name."

"Why not? Everybody else has a real name."

"Because, when you were born, you were such a perfect baby girl that your father and I could not find a name perfect enough for you. We decided to let you choose your own."

I was not surprised. My parents often said that I was a "perfect" child. It irritated me but I was used to it. It was very hard being perfect and to do everything my parents expected me to do, especially since they very seldom told me what that was—it seemed as if I was supposed to know what was the thing to do, without being told.

At first, they had called me **Poodle** because my nose turned up like a poodle dog's, they said. As I grew, my name became **Pooh** because the Winnie-the-Pooh stories were my favorites and, like Pooh Bear, I loved sweets.

The idea of choosing my own real name was exciting! I chased after my mother, who had turned and was walking down the hall.

"Where can I find a book of names?"

"Look in the dictionary. There are lots of names there."

I ran up to my father's desk. Careful not to disturb the papers, small tins of paper clips, his pipe stand, and rubber bands about the desk, I stood on his chair and reached across the table for the big, heavy dictionary. My father could not see very well, especially at night, and it would make him very angry if anyone moved anything, even an inch to one side, from where he had put it. He knew where everything was on that desk.

It was getting dark in the room, there were no electric lights. It was World War II in the Philippines, and the country was under occupation by the Japanese Army. I took a candle in its bottle and lit it carefully, being sure no wax would drip on the thin, wispy pages of the old dictionary as I knelt over it on the floor. Outside, the *cicadas* were buzzing, and a dog barked down the street. The candle light sent shadows up along the dusty walls of the room, and the words on the pages were small, and quivered and flickered. I started with the A's, one by one. I knew what I was looking for—a name that meant pirates and ships, sails roaring across the stormy oceans. I wanted to go to sea, I wanted to be a pirate.

I was excited and in a hurry—I looked for all the capital letters, skipping quickly over boys names like **Aaron**, and strange names like **Abd-el-Kadir,** until I came to the first girl's name—**Abigail**. It sounded pretty. I tried to think how it felt to be Abigail. It didn't feel right. Besides, it didn't have anything to do with pirates. I read on, running my finger down the pages. Nothing in the A's, although I stopped for a while to think when I got to **Arc, Jeanne d'**. Joan of Arc. How often I had gazed at the picture of Joan of Arc in one of my books—she was tied to a post, about to be burned up, with her face looking toward the sky. She seemed so brave. But no one would call me "Arc," they would call me "Joan," and that would not do at all. This was going to take me all night, and I knew that my father wouldn't let me waste candles. He would say "why can't it wait until tomorrow?" But I couldn't wait—I had to have my name that night.

I got to the B's and found it—**BARBARA**, feminine of **barbarus**, foreign, strange. As I read the words, I knew this was me. **Barbarian** seemed almost the same thing as pirate. "Foreign, strange" would explain why I was not like other children, why they threw stones and mud at me, why they yelled at me, *"mestisong bangus, madaling maubos!"* which literally translated means "you half-white fish, quickly eaten up" and is meant to be derogatory. My father was Filipino, but my mother was Irish-English and had grown up first in British South Africa and then in the United States of America. I was half white, and because of that, a foreigner, a stranger in my own country. It did not help matters that I hardly ever wore a dress, mostly shorts or overalls and a cotton shirt, and did not behave in a way that little Filipino girls were supposed to behave.

My family seemed different from the other families around us. One difference was that we didn't have any relatives. Other children seemed to have grandparents, uncles, aunts, and cousins around. But not us. I had one grandfather, my mother's father who was still alive and lived in Canada, but he did not want to have anything to do with us; he hadn't liked the idea of my mother

*marrying someone who had brown skin and when she
did, by eloping to the Philippines with my father, he never
communicated with her again. I often wished I had relatives; I thought that the word "cousin" had the nicest
sound.*

*Another way our family was different was that we
didn't belong to any religion. In the Philippines, most
people are Catholics. Almost everyone went to church
on Sundays, and knew how to pray the Rosary. Once, I
asked my father what we were, since we weren't Catholics. He said we were "freethinkers;" I didn't know what
that meant except that we didn't go to church, and we
didn't pray.*

*The biggest difference about our family was that my
mother was a "white" woman, and we children were
called "mestiso" (mixed race). This was not a good thing
to be in the Philippines unless you were rich, which we
weren't. I wasn't usually bothered by our family being
different except when other kids would call me names
or throw stones at me. My father said that people of
mixed races were often more intelligent than other
people, and that persons who married into their own
families had stupid children. I didn't know whether to
believe him or not, but sometimes, when he said it, I
would feel better.*

Barbara—strange, foreign. I had found my name. I
put the dictionary back exactly where it had been on my
father's desk, blew out the candle, and found my way in
the dark to the front porch. My parents were sitting in
the wicker chairs—my father silently smoking his pipe,
my five-year old brother asleep on my mother's lap. My
sister, Snuffy, who was eight years old, was sitting on
the top step holding one of her cats.

The mosquitoes attacked me immediately—they

were worse out here than inside the house—but I was used to them.

"I found my name," I announced.

"What name?" my sister asked.

"My real name. I want my real name to be **BARBARA.**"

"Why Barbara?" asked my mother.

"Because it means barbarian, like a pirate."

"It's a nice name," said my mother. Everyone was quiet after that. Maybe everyone was thinking. I wasn't thinking—I was just feeling proud and all puffed up.

After a while, my mother said, "Could I add something to your name? A long time ago there was a lady who was very nice to me; I thought the world of her. She is a doctor and lives in San Francisco, in California. Her name is Ann Purdy. It would make her very happy to know that you have her name. Can you add Ann after Barbara?"

I sounded it in my head. Barbara Ann. It sounded very nice. It sounded like the two names were meant to go together.

I was feeling very expansive—"Yes, that can be my name."

And so it was. Some years later, it became legal when I had to have a passport. The passport was my mother's, and had her name on it—Doreen Barber Gamboa. Also on the same passport was Snuffy's real name, Phylita Joy, and my brother's name, Spencer Comte. My sister had been named after my father, Felipe (my mother called him Philip). My brother was named after two philosophers, Herbert Spencer and Auguste Comte, but we all called him Trotsky because my father said he was "very revolutionary." There had been a Russian named Leon Trotsky who had helped lead Russian workers in a revolt against the Russian Czar around 1917, and was later assassinated. My father admired Leon Trotsky very much.

2

Chickens and Children

My parents considered themselves to be "leftists". This didn't mean that they were left handed. As far as I could tell, this meant that they wanted to change the world so that there would no longer be any poor people or rich people—everyone would have the same amount of money for what they needed. This made great sense to me but I didn't understand why it wasn't that way already. My father would try to explain it to me but it was too complicated and I didn't pay very much attention when he was doing his explaining. I was more interested in his chickens, and in all the stuff he had in his boxes.

My father's study was filled with tins and small boxes of things such as paper clips, rubber bands, metal washers and rusty screws, old keys, string, wire, and pieces of shoe leather (a "tongue" cut from an old leather shoe makes a perfect sling to hold the stone in a slingshot). He would let me rummage around in his boxes if I needed a small piece of anything; I would almost always find it or a substitute. He never threw anything away and sometimes on rainy days, I would sit on the floor of his study and investigate his boxes which were piled one on top of another. Once, I found an old bottle that had a

little dried up white shoe polish in it. I added some water to it and shook it up. The liquid looked like milk, so
Snuffy and I fed it to our dolls. We made a mess and
some of the shoe polish milk never came off the dolls'
clothes.

It was not always easy to find food for our dolls.
One day, we were playing house indoors and didn't want
to mess up the doll dishes with mud and grass; cut-up
pieces of paper didn't look very appetizing. Then my eye
spotted just the thing – the fringe on my mother's silk
shawl that was draped over a big black trunk in the hall-
way. We knew those fringes very well because we would
often try to braid them but they were so silky that the
braids never held. The fringe would make perfect *pancit*
(rice noodles), my sister and I agreed. I ran to get the
scissors and we cut enough of the fringe to give the doll
family a great pancit dinner. But when we put the shawl
back on the trunk it looked funny, no matter how we
arranged it. So we tried to even the sides by cutting off
more fringe. It was much better. So we thought, until
our mother noticed it later. I don't know how she knew
we were to blame but she was very angry at us and said
that from then on, until we learned when and where to
use scissors, we were not allowed to use them. This
caused us much disappointment because we were plan-
ning to give haircuts to the dolls.

My father had a chicken coop with some Rhode Island Red chickens that he was using for "experiments."
He said he was studying how chickens behaved, especially roosters toward each other and towards hens, and
how hens behaved when there was a rooster around.
His chicken coop was divided up into compartments, and
he would try to explain to me why he was "segregating"
one young rooster from the others, or why he put two
roosters in together. He had a black notebook in which

he would write down his "observations." His writing was very difficult to read; it always looked like scribble scrabble.

I didn't understand my father's chicken experiments but I liked Betty, the only chicken that had a name. We children were not supposed to pet any of the chickens because it would "ruin" his experiments, my father said. But Betty was different; she was not part of the chicken experiment, so we could pet her all we wanted. She was not kept in the chicken coop except at night; she could wander into our house anytime, and she always looked for my father so she could sit on his shoulder. She was a very fat chicken, but she could fly up to his shoulder or onto his desk. She never walked all over his desk, or messed up his papers. She would sit at one edge. My father never yelled at Betty, although he would often yell at the rest of us.

My mother didn't seem too interested in the chickens. She was interested in children, any children. When I was little, before the war began, she started a nursery school and kindergarten as part of a larger college in Manila. Young women who were studying to become teachers came to her school to learn about children and to practice teaching children. I started at her nursery school when I was less than two years old; every year I watched some of my schoolmates graduate to first grade and wondered why I was never included. Eventually, I did graduate to first grade when I was seven years old, having spent more than five years in nursery school and kindergarten! The way one could tell if you were ready for 1st grade was if you put one arm directly over your head and your hand could cover your ear on the other side of your head.

Several of the nursery and kindergarten children from my mother's school lived with us during the week, and sometimes even on weekends. One thing that we children liked to do was to listen to "The Hall of the Mountain King" from a phonograph record played on my mother's Victrola. We would take turns cranking the handle of the Victrola that made the record go around and around. The music started when the Victrola arm with its needle was put on the record as it was turning. If we had not cranked the Victrola long enough, the record would turn slower and slower, making the music sound lower and lower and wavier and wavier until it stopped. We giggled and laughed when this happened because the music sounded so strange; sometimes we would not wind the Victrola enough on purpose, just to hear the change in the sounds of the music as the record slowed down.

We also liked to pile into the Ford car at night and ride to the Santa Cruz bridge to see the man in the flying trapeze. There was a billboard near one end of the bridge and on it was a man in a flying trapeze in colored neon lights. The neon man would fly from one end of the billboard to the other, between two swings, and do a somersault in between. It was an advertisement for Yco Floor Wax. We never got tired of seeing it.

Having other children living with us was just the way it was but sometimes it was hard to share my books and toys with them, especially since there were never enough blocks to go around. One of the children was a little boy called Nippong, and whenever I tried to take my things back he would get angry and bite me on my arm—his bites would hurt! Once, Nippong bit Trotsky who was then about two years old. Trotsky picked up a heavy school bell by its wooden handle and before anyone could stop him, he whacked Nippong on his forehead with the sharp metal edge of the bell. It caused a gash on

Nippong's forehead that bled and had to be closed with stitches. I can't remember for sure, but I think Nippong stopped biting people after that.

People on foot jumped on the running boards of
our car, and on the back and on the roof. We kept
on going, driving very slowly on the flat tires.

3

Open City

World War II had started in Europe around 1939. On one side of the war was Germany, Italy, and their friends (called the Axis Powers), and on the other side was Great Britain, France, Russia and their friends (called the Allied Powers). The United States of America did not enter the war, on the side of the Allied Powers, until the Japanese bombed Pearl Harbor in Hawaii on December 7, 1941. Because the Philippines was then a Commonwealth of the United States, it meant that we, the Filipinos, were also in the war. I was seven years old and sitting at my school desk in the second grade that day, when the teacher said that we were to line up outside, that our parents were coming to get us, that a war had started.

The next day, December 8, the Japanese bombed Manila for the first time. My parents put us all under my father's big desk, covered up with all our mattresses. The house shook with each blast, and window panes shattered and crashed. It was much worse then all the earthquakes I had experienced up to then, and ever afterwards. I was startled by the loud noises but I don't remember being very frightened, perhaps because I didn't really know what it was all about except that we were in a war. My parents seemed very calm and so I was, too. After the first one, the air raids came like waves, with a quiet time in between that sometimes lasted for an hour, or hours. We never could tell how long before another air raid would begin, until we heard the faint rumble of the airplane engines that got louder and louder.

My father and some other men from the neighborhood dug a very deep and wide trench in the ground in between several houses and put a corrugated iron roof covered with deep earth over the trench. They brought wooden benches into the trench and, thereafter, during air-raids, we would run into that shelter carrying water. We filled all the containers we could find with water because my parents were not sure how long the faucets would have running water. It was dark and muddy in that trench, and crowded with people. One of them, Julian, always smelled very strongly of perfume.

Julian was our landlord; he owned the house we lived in, and we paid him money every month as rent. Julian was also a ballet dancer and would almost always wear a dress and high-heeled shoes or slippers covered with shiny sequins. He insisted that his name be pronounced "Julian," not "Hulian" as it is usually pronounced in the Philippines. My parents said that Julian didn't like being a man and preferred to be a woman, so he wore women's clothing, jewelry, and perfume. He also put on very red lipstick, had rouge on his cheeks, and eye shadow. He lived across the alley from our house on S. Fernando street, and sometimes my parents would send me to Julian's house with the rent money in an envelope (in those days, everyone paid cash for everything—there were no such things as checks or credit cards). Inside his house, or sitting on his upstairs balcony, Julian would wear a very brightly colored silk Japanese kimono. If I was on the street and saw him on his balcony, I'd wave at him and he would wave back. Sometimes he'd practice his ballet poses out on his balcony. The neighborhood kids would laugh at him, shout "bakla!" (meaning "sissy"), and throw stones at his house; I never did those things because my parents had told me that Julian's feelings were hurt by them. Julian sometimes came over to our house to collect the rent money himself, and he'd stay a long time talking to my parents.

Huddled together in that dark shelter, my parents would talk about taking us out of the city. Our house was in the south part of Manila in the Pasay district, near Nichols Air Base and Fort McKinley which were being bombed heavily by the Japanese. Once, during a lull in the bombing, my father took his bicycle to see what was happening in the city. He came back to say that all the grocery stores were being looted, people were evacuating the city, and the roads out of the city were jam-packed with cars and people trying to leave. He said it was terrible that people were looting and the police were doing nothing about it. He had stopped to watch the looting in one big grocery store; the Chinese owner was just standing there, even encouraging the people to come take the food for free. He saw my father watching and when my father refused to go into the store to take some of the groceries, the Chinese owner brought out a wooden case and gave it to my father, saying that it was better that the people take the food than to leave it for the Japanese. He had heard rumors that General MacArthur would surrender Manila. My father brought the crate home on the handlebars of his bicycle. It was a case of canned asparagus tips. All through the war, those cans of asparagus tips were very precious to us. We would open one on special occasions such as someone's birthday, or at Christmas, or when someone was very sick and couldn't eat anything else.

My father didn't want to leave our house with all our things in it. But after a bomb fell very close, sending everything crashing off the shelves with a deafening blast, and with shrapnel flying everywhere, he decided we had to go. We piled clothes, food, and water into our Ford car, locked the house, and started on the main road out of Manila going south.

My parents had some friends living in the town of Canlubang and that was where we were going. As we joined the crowds of people, cars, trucks, and horse-drawn caromatas heading south, people on foot jumped on the running boards of our car, and on the back, and even climbed on the roof. My father yelled at them to get off and that the car could not carry everybody, but no one paid any attention to him. I could hardly see out the car window because of all the people clinging to the car. By the time we got to the border of Manila, all the four tires of the car had blown out. But we kept on going, driving very slowly on the flat tires, all the way to Canlubang. We couldn't have gone any faster anyway, because the road was so packed with people and traffic.

On the way, as we passed near Camp Nichols, I saw many soldiers of the Philippine Army walking or crawling along the road with the rest of the crowd. Some of the soldiers were covered with blood, some were bandaged, with blood seeping through the bandages. There was no way we could get out of the car to help them because of all the people clinging to the doors and windows. My father said we couldn't help them, anyway. I did not like seeing them hurt and bleeding, and that was the first time I began to be afraid of the war.

We finally reached Canlubang, and we stayed in a small *nipa* (thatch) house in the middle of a sugar cane field. I chewed sugar cane all day and drank goat's milk. After about two weeks, my father said we were going back to Manila. He did not want to leave our house alone too long. He had heard on the radio that General MacArthur had declared Manila an "open city" and was leaving for Bataan with the U.S. and Philippine armies. "Open city" meant that he had surrendered Manila to the Japanese. The Japanese stopped their bombing and would soon be entering the city. There would be no fighting in Manila. My father felt it would be safe for us to go back.

We had enough gasoline left in the Ford car to make it back to our house in Pasay. The tires were still flat, of course, but no one was hanging onto the car this time. Everything in the house was as we had left it, except that our Rhode Island Red chickens were gone. We were very sad about losing Betty. We cleaned up the broken glass in the windows and inside the rest of the house, but there was nothing we could do about the shrapnel holes in the walls (shrapnel are thick pieces of metal that fly through the air with great force when a bomb explodes).

My father left the house to buy some food. We had brought food back with us from Canlubang, but it would not last very long. That week, he exchanged our car and the icebox (an old-style refrigerator) for nine sacks of rice. There was no electricity or gas, but we still had running water. Everything seemed very quiet, not just in our house but all over the neighborhood. My father said everything was very quiet all over the city. Everyone seemed to be waiting for something. It wasn't long before I found out what the wait was for—the Japanese Army entered Manila.

It happened in the afternoon. All the people, including us, went to the main road, Taft Avenue, and watched the Japanese soldiers march along the street. I was peering through an opening in one wall along the street.

No one among the people standing beside the road made any sound, except occasional murmurs to the person standing next to them. I could hear only the clop, clop, clop of marching soldiers. I could barely see, because there was so much dust, but I could hear.

Walking back to their houses, people were talking to each other. The war wouldn't last more than six months, they were saying. MacArthur would get reinforcements at Bataan and recapture the city.

General MacArthur did not come back until four years later. He had to surrender Bataan and Corregidor to the Japanese, and leave the Philippines. The President of the Philippine Commonwealth, Manuel Quezon, and the Vice-President, Sergio Osmena, also left the Philippines and fled to Australia to escape the Japanese.

General Edward King and General Jonathan Wainwright, along with about 60,000 American and Filipino army troops, were captured by the Japanese Army and sent to a prisoner-of-war camp. About half of the soldiers died along the way because of infected wounds, sickness, hunger, lack of water, and other causes. The long walk of 104 kilometers (about 65 miles) from Bataan to the prison camp became known as the "Bataan Death March".

4

The Rabbit That Wasn't

After things had quieted down in the city, the Japanese government opened up the schools again, and all children had to go to school. Our schoolbooks had to have a purple colored stamp mark in Japanese writing, to show that the Japanese had approved the books. We had gotten used to the Japanese being our conquerors; we had gotten used to doing the morning gymnastics exercises (*Radio Taishio*) that everyone had to do—listening to the exercise instructions, music, and counting (in Japanese) over the radio. One never knew when the Japanese soldiers would check your house unexpectedly to be sure you were doing the exercises.

In the third grade we were learning how to speak Japanese (*Nippongo*, it was called). I liked learning this new way of speaking, but I got tired of the short sentences we had to memorize and recite all together. My mind would wander during these recitations and I would daydream that I had a schoolbag like some of my classmates had—brown leather, with two straps and buckles that closed, and a handle. My schoolbag was made of straw, and had handles, but it couldn't close and didn't have straps or buckles.

One morning before school, our family was just finishing breakfast, and I asked my father if I could have a leather schoolbag. "No," he said, "they are too expensive and, besides, you have a bag."

"I don't like my bag. I want a leather bag like my friends have," I said, knowing with a sinking feeling that my father would continue to say no.

"Don't annoy your father, Pooh." My mother, as usual, was trying to prevent a blowup of my father's temper at the breakfast table. *Don't annoy my father? My father seemed to be annoyed almost all the time. Everything annoyed him—if the newspaper wasn't delivered at the exact time it was supposed to be; if his water glass was not placed exactly where it should be at the upper right hand corner of his place at the table; if his toast was burned by accident. Our toaster wasn't a pop-up one. It had side doors that you had to open when you thought the toast was ready, turn the bread over, and toast the other side the same way. My mother always made the toast at the table, but sometimes she would be so busy talking that she'd forget the toast. We kids would have to scrape the burned parts off and eat our toast but she would make a better one for my father. This made him mad because it was wasting bread, so my mother would scrape the burned parts off the burned slice and eat it herself.*

My father was more than annoyed at me this particular morning—he was angry and practically shouting. "Just because your friends have something doesn't mean you have to have one! A gunny sack can do just as well!" I wasn't afraid when my father got angry—I was used to it. Sometimes, I would just get angry right back. And this was one of those times.

"Well, then, I WILL use a gunny sack!" I stormed out of the dining room into the kitchen where a pile of gunny sacks was stored behind the back door. They were smelly and damp, but I pulled one out and ran to get my straw bag. I dumped everything from the bag into the gunny sack, and everything disappeared down to the bottom. Gunny sacks are very big—they can hold two small children. I twisted the top of the sack and dragged it through the house and out the door, where a horse-drawn *caretella* was waiting to take us children and my mother to school, where my mother was the kindergarten teacher. I shoved the gunny sack of my things under the seatboard of the caretella, then sat on the board. All the way to school, the caretella swayed and bumped along the broken pavement of the road that had been torn up by the bombing. As the horse clopped along, with the driver making clicking sounds at it, I felt less and less angry. I began to feel a little panicky, instead. What was I going to tell my friends about this smelly old gunny sack? I wished that I didn't have to go to school.

At the school gate, I jumped down from the caretella, my mother handed me the gunny sack, and without saying a word to her, I walked quickly across the playground toward my classroom, trying to lift the sack off the ground. But it was too big for me—I had to half-drag, half-lift it bumpily along the playground.

"Pooh, *TEKA*" (in the dialect, this means "WAIT!"). Several of my friends were calling to me. They caught up with me at the door of the classroom. "What's in the sack?" they asked.

"A rabbit," I said. I don't know why I said that. It just came out.

"Let's see it!" my friends were excited.

"No, it might jump out if I open the sack," I said.

I rushed into the classroom to my desk and shoved the sack under it. "Let's go play *piko* (a game like hopscotch) before the bell rings." We all ran outside and they forgot about the rabbit.

All the rest of that day, until the going-home bell rang, I spent hiding that sack of my books and papers under my desk. Everytime the teacher would tell us to get out a book or paper and pencil, I would have to look around to be sure no one was watching me when I bent over to find something in that sack. It was a very bad day for me because of that sack under my desk.

When I got home that afternoon, I put my books back in my straw bag and put the gunny sack back behind the kitchen door. The next day, I went to school with my straw bag. I never asked for a leather schoolbag again. In fact, I didn't need any kind of schoolbag soon after that, because my father decided to move us out of the city into the foothills of Rizal Province. I did not go to school again until high school, many years later.

Leoncio would let me go into his house and play
with the puppies.

5

A Room of My Own

My father's decision to move us out of the city into
the foothills was based on his prediction that it wouldn't
be too long before the city ran out of food. Or, he said,
General MacArthur would return and there would be
bombing again. He didn't like the idea of being trapped
in the city if the Japanese or the Americans destroyed
the bridges and roads connecting the city with the prov-
inces. I was ecstatic about moving, because I had sometimes been to the foothills when I was small and had
longed to live there. There were only a few houses, no
paved roads, with fields of grass, creeks, and hills that
seemed like mountains to me. It smelled so good in the
foothills, especially early in the morning. And early in
the morning there were little spider webs across the
tops of the grass like small flat roofs, with tiny beads of
dew stuck onto the webs that sparkled in the early morning sunlight. My father said we would plant vegetables
so that we could always have food. And we could have
chickens and ducks.

My mother didn't seem too happy about moving. It
was too far from Manila for us children to go to school.
She and my father would continue to commute to their
work in the city by caretella and on foot (a trip of about

two-three hours each way), which meant that we children would be left alone all day until they got home late at night. I was to be in charge of Snuffy and Trotsky. It sounded very good to me—no school, no memorizing Nippongo sentences, and—best of all—being out in the fields and creeks where I could fly kites, make rafts, and feel the wet grass in the mornings between my toes, while I tried not to step on the shining spider roofs.

But there seemed to be no vacant house for us in the area of the foothills around the town of San Juan where my father had decided we should go. Every weekend my parents would make the trip and look for a house. I was hoping they would find a house big enough for me to have a room of my own. I shared a room with my sister, two ladies who worked with my mother in the kindergarten school, and several other children who boarded with us during the week while they went to the kindergarten. I was glad that all these other people were not going to move with us except for one of the ladies, Dote, who had become part of the family.

One weekend, my parents found a house at last! It was vacant, they said, because it had been looted of all the water pipes, window shutters, and wiring. The house was just walls, floors, and roof. I didn't care about all that—"Can I have a room of my own?" That was the important part.

"No," my mother said, "there are only two bedrooms. But there is a very big yard right next to a huge empty field, and a *ratilis* tree." She knew I loved to eat the small red fruits of the ratilis tree. It wasn't a good climbing tree, though, because the branches were brittle.

We moved all my father's books, all the beds and furniture, all the pots and pans, and everything else in caretellas because there was no gasoline to run any trucks. Gasoline was available only for Japanese army vehicles, and for a few cars belonging to rich people and "collaborators." Collaborators were people who helped the Japanese Army and got rich doing it. Nobody liked collaborators but years later, after the war had ended, my father said that the Japanese Army would have made life much more difficult for the people if it were not for the influence of a few of the collaborators who had helped the Japanese run the government.

From the very first time I saw our new house, Number 75 on Ortega Street, I loved it. It was a wooden house with a rusting corrugated iron roof. Bougainvilla vines, old and gnarly but with hundreds of purple flowers, twined around the front porch. The vines hung across a narrow path to a broken-down arbor that once must have been quite elegant—there were remnants of black and white ceramic tile showing through layers of dead leaves and dried mud under the bougainvilla. The house stood on the edge of a hill and looked like a one-story house from the front. The back of the house, however, went out over the hill, and there were two small rooms under the main house. To get to the rooms, you had to go out the front door and around the side of the house under the arch of bougainvilla, where there were steep, narrow stone steps that led down the hill to a side door. During the rainy season those stone steps were covered with slippery, green moss. Under the two rooms was a bottom level space that my father said could be used to keep chickens and ducks so we could have eggs. The back yard had a small pond filled with smelly dark water, and there were frogs among the plants around the pond. The water in the pond came mostly from the septic tank under the house and from rain, especially during the rainy season.

And there was the ratilis tree! It was very tall and blew wildly in the wind. On many hot afternoons I sat near the top of that tree and pretended that I was in the crow's nest of a ship sailing across the ocean and blown by the winds.

My father moved all his bookcases of books and his desk, papers, and boxes into one of the small rooms under the main house—that was his study. The other small room was for Dote. We children shared one bedroom, and my parents had the other bedroom in the main part of the house. The kitchen was very small and had a back door that my father nailed shut. Because the back stairs had also been looted, and the back part of the house stuck out over the hill, it would be a long fall down if anyone walked out the back door.

We lived in that house on Ortega Street for about four years. One day that I will always remember is the day I got a room of my own. It was one of the days I went to get a haircut from Leoncio. Leoncio was a chauffeur who no longer had a car to drive, so he earned money by giving haircuts to people who lived in the neighborhood.

My mother usually sent me to get a haircut on a Saturday afternoon, after Leoncio had gotten up after his siesta. It seemed to me that everyone in San Juan except me would take a siesta in the early afternoon when the sun was so blistering hot. *Siesta* is a time for taking naps, usually lasting two or three hours. I detested taking naps but I liked siesta time because it was so quiet and I could do anything I wanted to do except tease my sister. Whenever I teased Snuffy, she would cry loudly and wake my mother from **her** siesta, which would make my mother angry at me and she would sometimes whack my rear end with her slipper. So, mostly, I took a book up into the ratilis tree and read.

Leoncio's house was down the hill from our house, and I would run down the hill yelling "Leoncio! Leoncio!"

He would put his head out of a window and tell me to wait. Then he would come outside and set a high stool under the banana trees in the back yard of his small bamboo and nipa house, wrap a white cloth around me, and cut my hair with scissors that were very sharp and shiny. Sometimes he would ask me how my parents were, and if the duck or chicken eggs had hatched yet. But mostly he would just cut my hair. I liked getting my hair cut; my head would feel so cool and light afterwards. When he had finished, Leoncio would untie the cloth and brush off my neck with a very soft brush. Then he would let me go into the bottom floor of his house and play with the puppies. It seemed as though Leoncio always had puppies.

One Saturday, while I was playing with the puppies, I heard a sudden loud sound, sort of between a crash and a rumble. It seemed to come from the top of the hill where my house was. I ran outside to see Leoncio staring up the hill to my house. From that distance, I saw my mother run outside and around the house to the back. Leoncio and I ran up the hill and climbed over the broken fence into my back yard. My mother met us saying, "Your father's study has collapsed into the chicken coop! All those books must have been too heavy for this house!"

We went to the door of the study. One end of the floor had separated from the wall and had crashed down into the lower level, which was the chicken coop. The other end of the floor was still attached to the threshold on which we stood, so the entire floor was on a slope, and all my father's stuff had slid down against the back wall and piled up.

When my father got home, everyone including Leoncio, carried all the books and bookcases, desk, and boxes and papers upstairs into the living room, which

thus became my father's study. As I carried up the last
load of books, I looked at the empty room with its floor
sloping down into the chicken coop, and I had an idea.
This could be my room. I would put my straw mattress
on the sloping floor against the back wall so that I
wouldn't roll off at night. I could line up all my books and
cigar boxes of things on the beam that had once been
holding up the edge of the floor. There would also be
space on the beam for my little doll, Martha, in her small
wicker basket. I wouldn't be able to see out the window
by standing next to it because the floor had fallen too
far below it, but I could see the sky when I lay on the
sloping floor.

Full of excitement, I ran to my parents with my idea.
Yes, they both said—I could have my father's old study
for my room. Snuffy asked if she could sleep in my room
sometimes, too, and I said yes, feeling very generous.
She only tried it once and got scared because it was too
far from our parents' bedroom. But she often came during the day to play in my room, although everything we
played with ended up rolling down the floor to the chicken
coop.

All I had to do was sit up in the ratilis tree above
the clothes line. I could read, or pretend that I
was out on the open sea in a ship with sails
unfurled. . . .

6

Guarding the Clothes

It seemed to me that I had to do most of the jobs around our house. My mother explained that I was the oldest, and my sister and brother were too little. They were also sick very often so I didn't really mind the work except for one job that I really hated—doing the laundry.

Once or twice a week, my mother and I would take all the dirty clothes into the bathroom and wash them. The bathroom had white tile around the walls and on the floor, and when we first moved in, there was nothing else—no toilet, except for the hole in the floor where a toilet had once been, and holes in the walls where there used to be faucets and pipes. When the house was looted, all the bathroom and kitchen fixtures had been taken. My father found an old toilet somewhere, and he and one of our neighbors put the toilet where it should go. It drained directly into the septic tank.

None of the houses in the foothills had any water, so there was no reason to put in any pipes or faucets. My father and I would carry cans down the hill to an artesian well, line up with the rest of the people, fill our cans with water, and carry them back up the hill (those water cans were heavy!). When my father wasn't home, I would go by myself to the well and get the water. We poured most of the well water into a big old metal drum that was kept in the bathroom for flushing the toilet, doing laundry, and taking baths. To take a bath, you stood in the middle of the bathroom floor, dipped a can into the drum of water and poured the water over yourself. Then you took a bar of soap and soaped yourself all over. You rinsed all the soap off with more cans of water poured over yourself. During the rainy season it was easier and more fun – we kids would take most of our clothes off and run out into the hard rain carrying the bar of soap. We could stay out in the rain as long as we wanted, unless it was storming with thunder, lightning, and strong winds that might blow a tree over on you. In the dry season, it took many trips to the well to keep the big drum full and sometimes I would forget to check the water level.

In the kitchen we kept a smaller can of water for cooking and a red clay jar for drinking water. The clay jar kept the drinking water cool—the walls of the jar were porous and a little water from the jar would seep into the walls. This water would evaporate, keeping the jar cool. The water from the jar was delicious in the very hot, tropical weather.

Doing the laundry not only used up the water in the drum very fast, but the clothes (especially the bedsheets and my father's trousers) were heavy when they were wet. My mother and I would kneel on the hard bathroom floor with a low circular large tin pan (called a "*palanggana*") between us, scrub the clothes with huge bars of native soap, and then scrub and scrub the clothes against each other. This hurt my knuckles and hurt my knees. After the soaping and scrubbing, we would rinse and squeeze and wring the clothes several times, changing the water in the pan each time. Then we carried the rolled wet clothes outside and hung them to dry in the hot sun, with the wind making them dry faster. At noon the sun was hottest, and since I did not take siesta, it was my job to guard the clothes while they dried on the line, to be sure no thief would sneak over the fence and take them.

You see, during the bad times of the war, almost everyone was poor and some people had absolutely nothing so they had to steal. But if they stole our clothes, we had no other clothes ourselves, so the clothes had to be guarded. That was a job I liked because all I had to do was sit up in the ratilis tree above the clothes line. I could read, or pretend I was out on the open sea in a ship with sails unfurled, sitting in the crow's nest and keeping my eyes peeled for enemy ships. My name was "Jack" and the captain of the ship was always asking me if everything was all right, and I would answer, "Aye, aye, sir!" And no thief ever tried to steal our clothes.

One hot, quiet afternoon, I was up in the ratilis tree guarding the laundry, when I heard a faint yell in the distance, calling *"Magnanakao! Magnanakao!"* It meant "Thief! Thief!" It was a neighborhood call for help. When anyone heard that cry, even during siesta, they would rush outside to help catch whatever thief was stealing a neighbor's things. It seemed that there were always more thieves during siesta time; I guess the thieves knew almost everyone would be asleep.

I heard dogs barking, and the cries got louder and louder. I stood up as tall as I could in the tree to look across the fields and hills, and in the distance I saw a crowd of people and dogs chasing a man who was carrying something under his arm. He and the crowd were heading in the direction of the path just below our hill, and I knew instantly that the way to catch that thief was not to follow the crowd but to go the opposite way around the hill, then head up the path **toward** the thief.

I rushed down the tree with my heart beating fast with excitement and with the certainty that I was going to catch that thief. I ran through the fields and down the hill, and made the turn up the path. Sure enough, there was the thief running full steam toward me, with the people running after him. I stopped right in the middle of the path, my heart beating faster, suddenly not knowing what I was going to do when this big man would reach the same spot where I was. As he ran toward me I could see that he was carrying a rooster under his arm—he had stolen someone's rooster. I suddenly heard someone in the crowd yell at me in the dialect, *"Bata, alis ka diyan! Alis ka diyan!"* ("Child, get out of there! Get out of there!"). But for some reason I just stood there. As the man came rushing at me, I held out my arms. He was panting very hard, his face sweating and his eyes wide. He shoved past me, putting the rooster in my hands, and ran on. I turned to watch him, the rooster in my arms, until he disappeared around the hillside. The people chasing him stopped when they got to me. Someone took the rooster from me and told me it was a very brave thing I did, but never to do that again—one never knew if the thief would have a knife.

I was very proud of myself as I trudged up the hill to my house—I had gotten a stolen rooster back. Someone must have told my father later because that night he was furious at me. He said the man could have hurt me. "No," I said, "the man wasn't going to hurt me, he only wanted the chicken, and he was scared of all the people running after him." My father said that I had no common sense, and if there was ever a thief in the neighborhood, I was to go in the house and stay there. I grumbled to myself about having to miss all the excitement in the neighborhood, but I always tried to do what my father wanted me to do—I didn't like listening to his bad temper.

-LEWI

7

My Father's Bad Temper

Everyone said that my father had a bad temper because he was a *Visayan*. This meant that he had been born in the Visayan Islands, a group of many small islands in the central part of the Philippines. There are three major parts of the Philippines: a big island to the north called *Luzon* where we lived, another big island on the south, called *Mindanao*, and the Visayan Islands in the middle. People born in the Visayan Islands, or coming from Visayan families, were said to have very bad tempers. I had never been to the Visayan Islands; you had to take a boat to get there. My father visited his old home town once in a while, and he would come back with dried, sliced bananas wrapped partly in a paper cone and dipped in sticky syrup. I loved these "sticky bananas," as I called them.

When my father got angry, he would practically explode. Everyone but me was afraid. I don't know why I was not afraid of my father—perhaps because he was sometimes funny, and he would tell us stories; my favorite of his stories was the "Adarna Bird." He would make shadow puppets with his hands for us on the wall at night, mostly animals. He could make a very good shadow duck, that quacked. When I was little, he would let me swing on his arm. He would sing while he was taking a shower. He would mostly sing a funny song—"it ain't gonna rain no more"—but sometimes he would sing a sad song— "just a-wearying for you."

I was about six years old when my father got angry at me for the first time. It was the day I had taken a hammer and cracked open my coconut shell bank. Snuffy and I each had a shiny coconut shell bank that had a slot on its surface for coins. My father insisted that we have "savings" for something we might want in the future. I didn't know what that something was, but when anyone gave me a coin, I slipped it into the slot in the coconut shell bank, just as my father told me to do. The shell was almost a perfect sphere. I often wondered how it was made—the insides of the coconut shell had to be all scraped out, made all shiny, and then closed up whole again except for the slot. The only way to get the coins out of that bank all at once was to crack the shell with a hammer. Then you could get a new coconut shell bank and start saving all over again.

The day that I cracked open my bank, I took all the coins and walked down the alley to the corner Chinese store where I spent all the money on boxes of wooden matches. It was siesta time so no one else was around, and I took those matches to our back yard stone cook-ing area and had a glorious time building little stick houses with the hundreds of matches and then setting them on fire. The little piles would burst into flame with great swooshing sounds. I was delighted, and so en-grossed in what I was doing that I did not notice my father come into the back yard with my brother, who was about a year and a half old. When my father saw what I was doing, he was furious. He stamped out the small fires with his big shoes and demanded to know where I had gotten the matches. When I told him that I had broken open my bank, he became even more angry about the "total waste of money." He was also angry and yelling about the Chinese store owner who was "stupid enough to sell all those matches to a small child!" I burst into tears, and when he had finished yelling at me, I ran underneath the house where there was a small dark crawl space. I huddled there, crying, until I felt a tiny hand gently patting me on the back. It was Trotsky, who had toddled under the house after me. "Poo booloon," he was saying, "poo booloon." He was trying to say "poor Poodle" but he couldn't quite pronounce my name.

My father's bad temper would always upset my mother. She would be especially upset if he got very angry in the middle of a meal. Then he would stand up, grab the tablecloth, and jerk it suddenly to one side so that all the dishes and food would crash onto the floor. My mother would run out of the room, crying, and we children would just sit there until my father stomped out of the room. Then we would quietly pick up the dishes and clean up the floor. Most of our dishes were chipped or cracked because of my father's bad temper. We never had any glasses for water. We used enamel cups. I could not understand why my father would do this except that he had a bad temper. My mother was very different— she never liked fighting or shouting, and she always tried to make things nice for everyone. Whenever she and my father had a fight, she would go off into another room and cry. I would find her and try to make her feel better, stroke her hair, or let her hold onto me until her crying stopped.

My father's bad temper would sometimes make my mother worry. One day, after we had moved to the foothills, a Japanese sentry house was put at the corner of our road where it intersected with several other roads.

From our front porch we could see the sentry house in the distance because there was nothing between our house and the intersection of the roads except fields. A Japanese soldier was usually standing in or near the sentry house, with a rifle and bayonet. Sometimes, a Japanese officer was there to make inspections. Notices were sent to all the houses that every adult had to bow to the sentry when they passed him. The bowing had to be done correctly, from the waist. Children did not need to bow, although it was good if they did. When my father read the notice, he blew up. He was not going to bow to anyone, he shouted, not even to the Queen of Sheba.

The Queen of Sheba, whoever she was, was always used in our house to mean some great being. For example, when Snuffy would pout and refuse to do something, she was called the Queen of Sheba. When I would tell her to go get something for me, she would call me the Queen of Sheba. Once, Snuffy and I dressed Trotsky up as the Queen of Sheba. We draped my mother's lace tablecloth over his head, and put on him my mother's pearl necklace and earrings, and her bracelets. We sat him on a chair that we put on top of the dining room table, and we bowed to him, and he ordered us around. The only trouble was that he had the whooping cough, and every time he had a coughing and whooping fit, all his finery would fall off, and he almost fell off his throne.

When my father said he wasn't going to bow to any sentry, my mother was worried: "Phil," she said, "you'd better bow, or you can go around to the other side of the hill to get home." My father asked why he should go the long way around to get to his own house? My mother pleaded with him until he agreed to take the long way.

One day, however, he did not take the long way. I saw him in the distance as he approached the corner of our road leading past the sentry house. I hoped the sentry was somewhere in back and wouldn't see my father. I began to run along the road toward the corner where the sentry post was, and saw that the sentry was there as usual. I saw my father walk past him and he did not bow. I saw the sentry yell something at him and call him back. My father turned back and began to yell at the sentry. As I got closer, I could hear my father; his temper was up, and he was refusing to bow. He was giving the sentry a lecture about why he was not going to bow to any person, not even to God, if there was a God. The sentry aimed his bayonet right at my father's waist just as I ran up to them. But my father did not seem to notice the bayonet, nor me. Nor did he stop his lecture, with full anger, at this Japanese soldier, who was beginning to look puzzled. He turned, went into the sentry house, and came out with a Japanese officer. My father did not bow to him, either, but started explaining more calmly to the officer why he was not going to bow, not even to God. At the end of all this, my father did not have to bow. In fact, he was the only person in the whole neighborhood who was allowed to pass that sentry without bowing for as long as the Japanese were in our neighborhood. So he never had to take the long way home again. After that, he always said it was an example of how one could get his way just by "reasoning" with the other person; one did not need weapons. My mother said it was not reasoning at all—the Japanese were just afraid of my father's bad temper because it was worse than any weapon.

"Your punishment is to rip off all the pockets on your shorts!" Miss Behenna was clear and emphatic.

8

Miss Behenna

While my parents were at their work in Manila during the day, I was in charge of Snuffy and Trotsky. Sometimes I also took care of one or two other little children who boarded with us. These were children whose parents had been wanted by the Japanese for anti-Japanese activities, and they had to go into hiding. They had asked my parents to take care of their children until they could send for them. The children were younger than I and they never gave me any trouble, so it wasn't hard taking care of them. One was a little boy named Boybie; the hardest part of taking care of Boybie was having to boil his clothes. He had a skin disease called "impetigo" and my mother insisted that his clothes be put into a big can of water on the fire and boiled.

Snuffy always helped with the little kids except when she couldn't get her way, and then she would pout. When she pouted, I usually let her have her way. We would build houses out of the furniture and bed sheets, or play school, or hide and seek. I would read Winnie-the-Pooh stories to the others, and stories from a big book called "Children's Literature." This book had no pictures but the little ones would listen very quietly. They liked fairy tales but I didn't like them very much—fairy tales seemed to be mostly about three brothers, or three sisters, and the oldest one was always the worst and the youngest one was always the best.

I made a set of playing cards out of blue cardboard, drawing the faces and numbers with the hearts, spades, diamonds, and clubs, and taught the others how to play rummy and black jack. I had learned these games from one of our neighbors, and I wished I could have a pack of the shiny colorful playing cards with designs on the backs. The cards I made were all right, although eventually the cardboard started to crease and bend with all the playing, and we could almost guess which cards were which, just by the creases and tears on the backs. Actually, it was only Snuffy and I who could add up the numbers on the card faces, but we let the little ones hold some cards and they never knew they weren't really playing. Small children who were allowed to join the older children's games without really playing were called "*saling pusa*" (in the dialect it means "a cat that joins"). No children ever wanted to be "saling pusa," so they weren't supposed to know. By the time a child began to realize that he or she was only "saling pusa" and would strenuously object, he or she would have learned enough about the games to really play.

Every once in a while, my mother would worry about leaving us alone. One day, she brought a lady to our house. Her name was Miss Behenna, and she was a Quaker. I didn't know what that meant. My mother explained that it was a kind of religion, like being a Catholic. My mother said Miss Behenna was going to come every morning and stay with us for an hour or so. I didn't like that idea at all. I was taking care of the little ones without any trouble and I didn't like anyone telling me what to do. Grown-ups, except my parents, always seemed to be telling me what to do! I liked it even less after the first day she came and ran her finger over the piles of newspapers that my father kept stacked on the living room floor along the walls. Ever since his study floor fell into the chicken coop, he had to keep his newspapers in the living room. He never threw any of them out even after he finished reading them because he was keeping them to clip out articles he needed for a book he was going to write someday.

Miss Behenna said the newspapers were dusty and that I was to dust them everyday. Then she asked me what we did all day, and I told her about schoolwork assignments that my mother left for us to do, the play houses, and hide and seek, and about the cards. She said that we should be learning something useful, and that she was going to teach my sister and me how to knit. The next day she brought knitting needles and yarn, and began to teach us about knitting.

At first, I was eager to learn; I had never seen my mother knit, and it was exciting to think that I could make something for her. Miss Behenna said I should start with something small, like socks for my brother. She wanted me to keep working on the socks even when she wasn't there; every day she would inspect the progress of the sock, in addition to the dust on the newspapers. It was slow going, especially since she would make me unravel everything I had done if it hadn't been done correctly. Pretty soon I got tired of knitting. The sock never seemed to grow any larger. Snuffy was knitting a shawl for her doll; she was good at it, and Miss Behenna would say what a nice job she was doing.

One afternoon, I decided to make a kite and needed kite string. I couldn't find any string around the house until I remembered the sock I was knitting and the ball of yarn that went along with it. I didn't think twice—I unraveled the sock and used the whole ball of yarn along

with the unraveled sock to fly my kite. It wasn't very
successful—the yarn kept breaking when I would just
get the kite started up. I would knot the pieces together,
but it would break in a different place. I finally decided
that yarn did not make good kite string and put the kite
away.

The next day Miss Behenna came as usual and asked
to see the progress on my sock. I told her that I had
unraveled the sock to use the yarn for my kite. She didn't
believe me, and I had to go get the kite and the knotted
lengths of yarn to show her. She was very angry. She
said she didn't like wasting her time, and I was a disobedient child and should be punished. I had never thought
I was disobedient—I always did everything my parents
wanted me to do.

"My parents don't want us to be punished," I said.

"Your mother gave me full authority, and your punishment is to rip off all the pockets on your shorts!" Miss
Behenna was clear and emphatic.

I was aghast! I needed those pockets. I needed them
to carry all the things I found whenever I was out in the
fields and creeks. I liked to pick up pretty stones, pieces
of metal, and dried seeds with curious shapes to bring
home. I needed the pockets when I climbed guava or
mango trees and picked the green fruits to eat later. I
needed the pockets to carry just the right kind of stones
for my *tirador* (slingshot) so that I could shoot back at
the neighborhood boys who threw rocks at me. I kept
the slingshot stones in a separate pocket so I wouldn't,
by accident, use one of my pretty stones.

I told Miss Behenna I needed the pockets. She said
I had to rip them off—she was not leaving until I did.
My mother had said to do whatever Miss Behenna
wanted me to do, so there was nothing else to do but rip
the pockets off my shorts. I hoped she would let me keep

the pieces of cloth because I knew I could sew them on later, but she insisted I hand them over to her. She put them in her purse.

When my mother got home that night, I told her what had happened and that I did not want Miss Behenna ever to come to our house again. I don't know what my mother said to her, if she said anything at all, but Miss Behenna never did come to our house again. Perhaps Miss Behenna, herself, told my mother she wouldn't be coming over again because I was so disobedient. I never found out which way it was.

"Play some more." The Japanese officer sat down.
I decided to let him stay, and played my violin for
him.

9

The Sad Japanese Officer

Everyday I practiced my violin. I didn't have a violin teacher but I had a book called "A Tune a Day" and it showed, in pictures, which notes corresponded to which finger positions on the four violin strings. I had always wanted to play the violin, ever since my mother took me to my first concert when I was about six years old. It was before World War II had spread to the Philippines. The concert was held in the Metropolitan Theater, a large pink building near one end of the Santa Cruz Bridge in Manila. It was a very special treat for me to go to a concert with my mother—it was about my only chance to have her all to myself.

The theater was full of people. My mother and I sat high up in the balcony. A man came out by himself on the stage and played the violin. I had never heard such beautiful music before. I sat very still, listening. When the man finished playing and everyone was clapping, I pulled at my mother's sleeve to get her attention. I pointed to the man and said, "I want to do that." My mother said she would see about it.

Some time later, after I kept reminding her, my mother brought me to an American missionary lady who was also a violin teacher. She tested me by asking me to hum each sound I heard when she struck certain keys of her piano, one at a time. Afterwards she told my mother I was "ready" to learn the violin, and I began taking lessons once a week at her house. She gave me the book, "A Tune a Day," to start. The lessons didn't last very long; a few months later, the war with Japan started and the American missionary lady had to leave. She gave me the violin to keep (it was not a full-size violin), and several other music books that followed after "A Tune a Day."

I loved the violin. By myself, I learned the third position from the music books. Many years later, when I started lessons again, I found that I had been doing many things wrong; it was hard work to unlearn all the bad habits I had gotten used to.

None of my family could stand my violin playing. Snuffy and Trotsky would put their hands over their ears and go somewhere else. My parents would gently suggest that I practice my violin during the daytime while they were away. So I did. Usually I practiced in the early afternoon, in our living room, while the others were taking their naps in the bedroom with the door closed. I couldn't practice in my own room because it was hard to balance on the sloping floor.

For some time, my favorite piece was "Santa Lucia." I would play it over and over. One afternoon, I was practicing that piece. It was extremely hot and dusty out on the road in front of our house, but it was also very hot inside so I left the front door wide open to let some of the breezes in while I was practicing.

Suddenly, I noticed a Japanese soldier come walking through our front gate. I stopped playing. He was an officer. I could tell because his uniform was starched and ironed very well; his black boots and the buttons on his shirt were shiny, and he had an officer's cap. But most important of all, he had a saber hanging from his belt. Regular Japanese soldiers did not have sabers or boots; they had cloth leggings wound part way up the legs of their trousers. The Korean soldiers wore uniforms that were sometimes torn and dirty.

The Japanese Army that invaded the Philippines included Korean soldiers. This was because Japan had conquered Korea in 1910, taking it over for themselves with the approval of the United States and major powers in Europe. The Koreans were considered inferior by the Japanese and were used as menial laborers; they were often mistreated. This was probably why, in many instances, the Korean soldiers were more cruel to the Filipinos than were the Japanese soldiers. My parents explained to me that, often, when someone is bullied, he turns around and bullies someone else. In our neighborhood, people were more afraid of the Koreans than they were of the Japanese. I was not afraid of the Koreans, I just felt sorry for them. Sometimes I would smile at them as I walked past them working in their vegetable fields; they never smiled back.

The Japanese officer stopped at the doorway and looked at me. "You can play the violin?" He spoke English very well.

"Yes," I said, "I'm learning."

"Play some more." The Japanese officer stepped across the threshold and sat down in a straight chair beside the door. I was hesitating whether to say he couldn't come in. My parents had told me never to let anyone in that I didn't know. But here was a Japanese officer. My parents never said what to do if the stranger was a Japanese officer. I decided to let him stay.

I played my "Santa Lucia."

"Play it again," said the Japanese officer. I did, and when I had finished and turned around to face him, he was crying. He was making no sound and was sitting very straight, but tears were coming down his face. He took out a handkerchief and wiped his eyes and blew his nose.

"How old are you?" he asked very quietly.

"Nine years old," I answered.

"I have a son in Japan who is ten years old, and he plays the violin also." His voice trembled a little, and it was very quiet. He took something out of his pocket to show me. It was a black and white photograph of a small Japanese boy in his school uniform. I looked at the picture and when the Japanese officer put it back in his pocket, I stood there looking at him, wondering if I should play some more for him.

"Play some more," he said.

I turned back to my music book and found some pieces to play. After I finished, he stood up and patted me on the head.

"Thank you," he said. "I will come back again soon. Be sure that you continue to practice. It is very important." He turned and went out the front door. There was a car stopped outside on the road in front of our house, and he got into it. The car drove away, making the dust in the road blow all over.

When my parents came home that night, I told them about it. They said I had made the right decision to let the Japanese officer come in and to play my violin for him.

Many afternoons after that, I waited for the Japanese officer to come back and listen to me play. But he never did.

10

The Spy

The Japanese Army built camps in some of the fields around our neighborhood; they also built storage areas for gasoline, oil drums and big crates of army supplies. Sentries always walked around the edges of these areas, which were surrounded by barbed wire. In one field, Korean soldiers planted vegetables; they would not allow any people near the vegetable field, which was also guarded. My father and I would sometimes take walks in the evenings along the roads beside the camps and storage areas.

It was always cooler outside in the evenings than inside our house, so the family would sit out on the porch, slap at mosquitoes, and watch the stars come out. Snuffy and I would look for the first star and make a wish. She and I would also keep our eyes on the sky, waiting for shooting stars.

Some evenings, my father would get up from his wicker rocker where he had been smoking his pipe, and say to me, "Let's go for a walk, Big." He called me "Big" because I was his biggest child. Another name my father called me by was "*Oo-sa*," the word in the dialect for "deer." He said it was because sometimes, I looked like a frightened deer. I had never seen a deer except in pictures, but he had seen many of them when, as a young man, he had worked as a lumberjack and cook in the forests of Oregon.

My father couldn't see at night because he had "night blindness," an eye disease. During our walks, every time we passed the Japanese camps and storage areas, I knew he would want me to count the tents, and the oil drums stacked up, and the crates. He also wanted me to remember where the piles of tires were stored and where the trucks were parked. He didn't want me to tell him out loud about all this; I was just to keep everything in my head. When we got back home we would sit at the dining room table in the lamplight, and I would tell him the list from my head while he wrote it down on a piece of paper using a code. I knew what this was for. My father was a member of "Marking's Guerrillas," a group of mostly men who lived in the mountains of Rizal province. Every so often, at night, some of them would quietly enter the Japanese camps all over the province and try to blow up the gasoline and oil drums and other stored material (this stealthy destruction of enemy property is called "sabotage"). To do this, the guerrillas needed information on the exact locations of the material and how much of it there was. It was my father's job to collect this information from the camps in our area. Because the Japanese sentries in our neighborhood knew about my father's night blindness, they didn't pay any attention to him and his little daughter who guided him in the evening walks. We walked slowly because he couldn't see, which gave me more time to count and remember where everything was.

Some nights, I would wake up hearing loud explosions and much commotion coming from the direction of the camps, and I knew some guerrillas had gotten through to do their sabotage work. The next day we could see smoke still coming from the burning camps, and we were glad. If the smoke was thick and black, we knew it was oil or gasoline burning. I never knew, until the war ended, how my father got the information to the guerrilla units in the mountains. It never occurred to me to ask him.

One night, someone came to our house. I was in my room downstairs under the house, almost asleep, when I heard the noise upstairs. I got up, went outside and up the stone steps into our house to see what was going on. I was too late; the person had gone, but my father was getting dressed and my mother was packing a small bag with some food. She was telling my father, "Take Pooh with you, you will never find your way in the dark."

Take Pooh where? I was getting excited.

"No," my father said, "I won't have to go, you'll see."

My parents were in their bedroom, and I watched as my father opened a bottom drawer where my mother kept her nightgowns, took out something heavy wrapped in a white canvas. I knew what it was, it was his gun. I had found it in that drawer sometime back, but had not told anyone; I just put it back.

"Phil, don't take that! If they catch you with it, it will be worse!" My mother sounded worried. My father said he was just checking it, he knew he would not need it. He put the gun back in the drawer. They both turned and saw me standing in the doorway.

My mother said, "Put on your clothes, Pooh (I was wearing my pajamas)—you may have to lead your father down the trapdoor and outside the back way." There was a trap door in my parents' bedroom that was covered with a small rug with a chair on it; the door opened down to my sloping bedroom. We never used the trap door, because there were no stairs. If anyone tried to get down it, they would have to jump through the door onto the sloping floor below. I went back to my room and changed my clothes. I was very excited, but also a little scared. Where were we going? Why?

All night we sat in the dark in the living room, waiting—I didn't know for what. I fell asleep in my chair several times. Finally, it was morning, and I woke up still in the chair. My parents were in the kitchen fixing coffee. It wasn't really coffee—it was dried corn that had been roasted and pounded into pieces, and mixed with some kind of tree bark. But my parents fixed it like coffee, and called it coffee, and drank it like coffee. I went into the kitchen and they smiled at me. They gave me some coffee in a cup, and this surprised me because I had never been allowed to have coffee before. I tasted it carefully, and it was very bitter. I didn't like it very much and drank only a little of it.

For the next two days my parents still seemed to be waiting for something or someone. My mother said not to go too far from the house except to get water from the artesian well. Then a man came to visit them, and they talked quietly in the living room for a while. After the man left, my father told me that everything was all right, that we wouldn't have to go anywhere, just like he had said. But he seemed very sad; I could almost see tears in his eyes. I wanted to know what had happened, but I knew I couldn't ask.

After the war ended, he told me about those two days. The person who carried the code about the Japanese camps and storage areas from my father to the guerrillas had been an 18-year-old girl, named "Nene." The night that I had been awakened was when a man came to tell my father that Nene had been caught by the Japanese, and that they were making her tell them the names of all her contacts in all the neighborhoods. The man had come to tell my father to get away as fast as he could. But my father had been very sure that Nene would never reveal the names of the people, like my father, who had given her information. He was right. Nene never told, and she gave her life so that others, including my father, would live. That was why my father was crying two days later when he was told about it. I never knew or even saw Nene, but I know she must have been very, very brave.

11

Alcohol and Tobacco

It was becoming harder and harder to find food. We hadn't had rice or bread for a long time. We had tried to plant vegetables in our back yard, but the ground was stony and the soil was thin. Sometimes we were able to harvest a few ears of corn, and *camote* (native sweet potato). We ate two meals a day, mostly green leaves of the *gabi* plant. With hardly any food to eat, my parents' physical condition was very poor; the two-mile walk uphill to our house from the corner where the caretellas dropped them off at the end of their long day, was utterly exhausting for them. They would get home bone weary, but always managed a smile and hugs for us. It would be dark before they got home. Snuffy and I would have supper waiting for them, the table set, and Trotsky and Boybie bathed and in their pajamas.

One night, my parents were later than usual. I kept looking out into the dark road, hoping to see them come up the walk any minute, but no one was there. I was getting really worried when I thought I heard my mother laughing outside the front door. I rushed to open it, and in stumbled my father, who fell across the threshold into the wastebasket that stood to the right of the door. His eyes were closed and he was not moving. I thought he was dead. I was rushing to him when my mother wobbled in, giggling and laughing loudly, tears streaming down her face. She could not stop giggling. I was truly frightened. Why was my mother laughing when my father was dead?

My mother must have seen the frightened look on my face, because she suddenly stopped giggling and told me not to worry, my father was alright, he was just drunk. She started giggling and laughing again, and my father was moaning and trying to get up off the floor. A strange smell permeated the room, sort of sweet, but it was making my stomach feel queasy. My mother was trying to help my father stand up, but she seemed very wobbly on her feet even after she took off her shoes. She said, in the middle of her giggles, that we needed to get my father to the bathroom and pour water on his head and face. Somehow, he, she, and I, got him to the bathroom, and I left both of them in there. I heard them washing, and I also heard them vomiting into the toilet, then washing some more. I was very frightened. I had never seen them like this before. I thought they were sick and were going to die. After a while, I heard my father go to his room and lie down on the bed. He slept all night, without eating any supper.

My mother took a bath, changed her clothes, and came out into the dining room. Her continuous giggling had stopped, but once in a while a giggle would slip out while she ate a little of her supper and tried to explain to us children what had happened. On their walk up the hills, it had been very hot, and they were exhausted. They had stopped to rest for a while in front of the gate of a rich neighbor, who happened to see them and invited them in for some refreshment. They gladly accepted and were served alcoholic drinks. On their empty stomachs, the alcohol went directly to their brains, and although my mother assured me they had taken only a little to drink, they had gotten "drunk." It made my father unsteady on his feet and almost unconscious by the time they got home, and it made my mother also unsteady on her feet and to have the fits of giggling and laughing. Vomiting, she said, was good because it got rid of any alcohol left in their stomachs. She said she was sorry if they had frightened us, but they had no idea that this would happen with just a little bit to drink. They had been so tired and thirsty, and the cold drinks had tasted so good.

That incident, the likes of which never happened again, turned me against alcohol in any form. I was ten years old, and determined that no alcohol would ever be drunk by my parents again. Before the incident, my father kept a bottle of native wine in a kitchen cabinet, and once in a while he would drink a *cupita* full, saying it was for "medicinal purposes." A cupita is a tiny glass, about two inches tall and an inch in diameter; in America, it is called a "shot glass." I took that wine bottle and emptied the contents down the sink. After that, when he would try to hide another wine bottle in the house, I would immediately find it and pour the wine down the sink. I checked the cupboards and dressers regularly. He knew that I was doing this, and he tried to explain to me the difference between getting drunk and having a few sips of wine. I could see no difference; they had told me that they had had only "a few sips" the night they had gotten drunk. One time I poured his wine down the sink while he stood there, waving his arms and angrily telling me to stop. I refused to stop. He did not try to take the bottle away from me. My father never used force with me; he always tried to "reason" with me. Reasoning did not help when it came to his wine because I could see no reason for getting drunk, and no reason for drinking wine.

My father smoked pipes and cigars for as long as I can remember. Mostly, he smoked his pipe. I grew to like the smell of pipe tobacco, and when I was little, I often begged him to let me pack the tobacco in his pipe. I didn't like the smell of cigars too much, but I liked getting the gold paper rings that were around each cigar. My sister and I would rush to see who could be the first to ask for the paper ring whenever my father took out a cigar. My mother smoked cigarettes. She made "smoke rings" for us by tapping her cheek with a finger while making an "O" with her mouth. We kids tried to put our fingers through the rings before they faded away. Although I sometimes begged her, she never let me try her cigarette. She said smoking was bad for children.

One day, I decided to smoke. I took one of my father's pipes from his pipe rack and went into the bushes at the side of our house, where I knew there would be plenty of dry leaves. I mashed up a bunch of dry leaves in my hand and stuffed the crumpled pieces into the pipe. I lit the leaves with a match and began to puff on the pipe as I had seen my father do. The fire kept going out, I couldn't get the leaves to keep burning. I gave up, put the pipe back, and decided to try cigarettes. I took several cigarettes from a package that was lying on top of my mother's dresser, and went back into the bushes with the matches and cigarettes. I put one cigarette in my mouth and lit it, as I had seen my parents do. It worked! The cigarette burned brightly as I sucked in, filling my mouth with smoke. I choked a couple of times, but was able to blow the smoke out. I did it again, several times, trying to make smoke rings. Then I began to feel funny, dizzy, and sick to my stomach. I stopped smoking for a while, then lit another cigarette to try again. I felt sicker and sicker, and almost vomited. I put the cigarette out and returned the unused ones back to the package on my mother's dresser. I was sick to my stomach almost all the rest of the day, and my mouth had a bad taste. I could not understand why anyone would want to smoke cigarettes. Eventually, because we had very little money, my mother stopped smoking and my father stopped buying wine.

They would suddenly rise up in flight, quacking like mad and flapping their wings.

12

Loka and Loko

Gabi plants grew around the little pond in our back yard. The water in the pond came from the septic tank under our house—the water was smelly and black, and the bottom of the pond was oozy (I fell in, once, trying to catch frogs). The pond was not good for wading, but the gabi plants grew very well. These plants had tuberous roots, each one like a huge turnip. The plants growing from those roots had long thick stems and large flat leaves that could almost be an umbrella in the rain; we boiled these leaves to eat. The gabi roots were dug up and either boiled and eaten or chopped up and dried in the sun or in front of the cooking fire. These dried roots could be stored and portions boiled up before eating. We didn't have a refrigerator (nor any electricity to run it even if we had one), and only food that was dried or salted could be kept for more than a day. Gabi roots don't have much taste, and are a little slimy. Gabi leaves and roots were all we had to eat for months and months.

The pond was also very good for ducks. We had two native ducks, colored black and brown, with white speckles and black beaks; one was female and the other male. They quacked and flapped their wings very noisily, and their one goal in life was to escape from our yard. It was my job to keep them from escaping, and if they succeeded, I had to go find them and bring them back. Because so many people were hungry, any ducks, chickens, or pigs that could be stolen or that strayed from their homes were sure to end up in someone else's cooking pot.

I thought those ducks were either stupid or crazy—why would they keep trying to escape? They had the pond full of small snails to eat, and a huge yard, and we weren't going to eat them because my mother needed the eggs. She was very thin by that time and often sick. So I named the ducks *Loka* and *Loko*, which means "crazy." To keep them from flying over the fence, my father would clip their wings while I held them one at a time. They would struggle to get loose and peck at me. I had to guide the scissors for my father so he wouldn't accidentally cut their skin. He couldn't see very well, but I was not strong enough to use the big scissors (which were very dull and rusty) needed for the tough duck wing feathers.

But their wing feathers would grow, of course, and I was never sure when they should be clipped again until I found the ducks gone and knew they had flown over the fence. I kept all the holes in the wire fence near the ground plugged with rocks, so there was no way they could get out of the yard except by flying.

When they got away, it was awful trying to find them. They could hear me call them—"EHHHHHK—YA! EEEEEEEE ITIKITIKITIKI!!," over and over—and they would hide in the tall weeds. I would stub my toes on rocks and stumble trying to find them in the dark of the early evening. I would stop to listen for the rustle of their feathers, or the *slurp, slurp, chip, chip,* sound they would make eating. Sometimes they would be right close to me, then suddenly rise up in flight, quacking like mad and flapping their wings. I would go chasing after them, yelling at the top of my lungs, furious. Sometimes I'd trip over a stone in the dark and scrape my shins. Once, I fell right on top of a piece of rusty barbed wire and tore a huge gap in one knee. When I did find them, I had to maneuver them home, chasing them toward our yard. They were always together—if I found one, the other would be there, too, which made it easy in some ways, but harder when it came to chasing them home. If one started off in the wrong direction, the other would follow. Sooner or later, I would get them home and lock them up in the chicken coop, saying mean things to them such as someday, if they weren't careful, they would end up cooked, and I would be happy!

There were times when I'd get really mad—I would be playing "kick the can" in the road with other kids, and Snuffy would run up to me and say, "Pooh, the ducks are gone!" I'd have to leave the game and go after those ducks.

Loka did not like laying her eggs inside the box of grass we put into the coop for her. She preferred to lay her eggs in the deep grass or weeds anywhere in our big yard, or over the fence if she got a chance. She usually laid one egg a day during the two weeks she was laying, so they weren't easy to find, and I had to be very careful where I walked so as not to accidentally step on one. I tried to spy on her many times, to see where she went to lay her eggs. Sometimes I could fool her, but most of the time she fooled me.

One day, there were more exciting things to think about than stupid ducks. It was January 9, 1945, my 11th birthday, and the Americans had landed in Lingayen Gulf on Luzon. That previous October, General

MacArthur had landed on Leyte, one of the Visayan Islands. The Americans were coming back. My parents heard the news on the short-wave radio that was run with batteries. Outside on the road in front of our house, I played with my birthday present of three marbles. I also got a small piece of sticky, raw sugar (*panocha*). I was ready to warn my parents if anyone was approaching. If I saw someone coming, I would throw a stone against the front door and my parents would hide the radio. They had to listen with their ears stuck right up to the radio because the sound was turned down so low. If the Japanese found out we had the radio, my parents would have been taken away. Snuffy and Trotsky did not know about the radio, but I did. My parents needed me to be their lookout, and no one would suspect that a little girl playing in the road was really a lookout. My mother whispered the exciting news to me after she called me back into the house.

Because it was my birthday that day, I could do anything I wanted to do, and everyone else had to do what I told them. That was the birthday rule at our house. My parents said they were going to fix a surprise for me, so I wasn't to come home until supper, just at dark, when the surprise would be ready. All the rest of the day I was very excited thinking about what the surprise could be.

I was away from home all afternoon, impatient for the sun to go down. When it did, I ran home. The house was dark, of course, but I could see the coconut oil lamp burning on the dining room table and all my family seated around, waiting for me. There was a delicious smell coming from the dining room. When I ran in, they all yelled, "HAPPY BIRTHDAY! SURPRISE!" My father's chair, where the birthday person was supposed to sit, was all decorated with *cadena-*

de-amor, a vine with pink flowers. The chair had arms, and when it was all decorated with the flowers, it looked very grand. But that couldn't be the surprise because we always did it that way on someone's birthday. Snuffy was jumping up and down, pointing at the table, and I saw the surprise. There, on our largest platter, were what looked like two roast ducks. Everyone was smiling at me. I was suddenly frightened. *Where did they get the ducks?*

Snuffy yelled out, "That's Loka and Loko! Now you won't have to chase them anymore!"

I burst into tears and ran outside and down the rock steps to my room. *No, no, no, they couldn't possibly have cooked the ducks! Why did they? Why did they?*

My mother came to my door and called me to come to her. She put her arms around me and said, "But we thought you hated those ducks! We wanted you to have something good to eat for a change, and we wanted to celebrate your birthday and the landing of the Americans in Lingayen Gulf. We thought you hated those ducks."

I was still sobbing. "No, I didn't really hate them. They just made me angry."

My mother patted me, saying, "You knew that someday we'd have to eat them. We all need meat very badly, your sister and brother especially. We're going to bring some to Mrs. Verdote, and to Leoncio. Everyone is starving and the ducks were going to be eaten sooner or later." I nodded my head, still sniffling. I knew she was right, but why did it have to be this way?

After I was sure they had finished supper, I went back upstairs. I had dried my eyes, and we sat on the front porch where we shared the piece of raw sugar.

It wasn't long after that before air raids started

again. This time, it was the Americans doing the bomb-ing. General MacArthur had come back to liberate us from the Japanese, just as he had said he would.

13

Manila is Burning

The American bombers came over us in "waves," day and night, just as the Japanese bombers had done in December of 1941. My parents always knew that the Americans would come to take the country back from the Japanese. "Six months more" was what I heard them say so often.

When General MacArthur landed in Lingayen Gulf on my birthday, my father said that we needed to build an air-raid shelter to be ready for the bombing by the Americans. He, Leoncio, and I started digging a trench along the side of the hill next to our house. My father said that the hill would be good protection for at least one side of the shelter. It was very difficult work because the ground was hard and had big rocks. The trench was only wide enough for one person, but long enough for five or six people to sit side-by-side in it. When the trench was dug, we started to build a roof over it, putting wooden rafters across, and covering the rafters with rusting corrugated iron sheets taken from the porch roof of our house. On top of the sheets we piled and compacted the soil and rocks that we had dug out of the trench. Before we had finished the roof, however, the air raids started. We had to finish the shelter in between the air raids, shelling by artillery, and machine gun fire from "dog fights" going on overhead. Dog fights were battles in the sky between American and Japanese fighter planes. Loud explosions, along with black puffs of smoke from antiaircraft guns were the sounds I heard most often above the steady roar of the bombers. At night there were also search lights that crisscrossed the sky.

Most of the bombing was taking place in and around Manila, and when the sirens sounded or when we heard the approaching bombers in the distance, we would head for our shelter. One night, we couldn't find Snuffy in our shelter—she had gone back to her own bed!

My mother would tell us to sing during the air raids, even at night when we were sleepy. We would sing "My Country Tis of Thee", "God Bless America," "Over There," and "Hail Columbia the Gem of the Ocean," as well as our national anthem, "Land of the Morning."

One day, some Japanese soldiers dug a machine gun nest right next to our air-raid shelter. There were usually three or four soldiers there all the time. They would fire their machine gun at American airplanes coming in low. The noise hurt my ears and I would cover them with my hands. This was the first time I saw my parents look worried. I knew what they were worried about—the Americans might try to wipe out that machine gun nest by bombing or strafing it, and we were right next to it. I found out later that they were also worried that the Japanese soldiers might turn the machine gun on us because they were losing the war. Once, one of the soldiers came into our shelter, tossing a hand grenade up and down in his hand. I was sitting next to the opening of the shelter, and he gestured to me that the whole shelter would blow up. We didn't say anything to him. We all sat very still, but my heart was beating very fast—I knew what a hand grenade was, and what it could do.

Another day, one of the soldiers came into the shelter holding out his army kit of rice. He gestured to us to take it. We hadn't any food, and we hadn't had any rice for more than a year. We took it saying, "*Arigato gosaimashta*", which means "thank you" in Nippongo. We were very hungry and eagerly stuffed the rice into our mouths with our hands, but it tasted sour and awful. My parents said it was spoiled and not to eat it. We buried it at the far end of the shelter so the soldier wouldn't know that we hadn't eaten it. We didn't want to hurt his feelings when he had tried to be kind to us. My father commented that the Japanese must really be having a hard time if their soldiers had to eat spoiled food. We would still sing our American songs during the air raids, but only in a whisper so the soldiers in the machine gun nest couldn't hear us.

After the incident with the Japanese soldier and the hand grenade, my parents decided that we children should be taken to a neighbor's air raid shelter for as long as the Japanese machine gun emplacement was next to our shelter. My father and mother would stay in our shelter so that the Japanese would not think we were afraid of what they might do. I didn't want to go, but I had to. In between the air raids, my mother took us up the road to the house of a wealthy Spanish neighbor. The house was very big, and was surrounded by a high stone wall lined at the top with shards of broken bottle glass so no one could climb over the wall. The air raid shelter in this house was a very large area underneath the house surrounded with concrete walls and painted white. Many people were in that shelter because the family was big and had many servants.

During heavy bombing, everyone would pray out

loud. The prayer would be the same, over and over, in Spanish—something like this:

"Dios mio, perdon, la consolacion, la consolacion..
Dios mio, perdon, la consolacion, la consolacion . . ."

They would also recite the rosary during periods between the bombing. All this chanting and moaning made me very nervous. I would much rather sing "Over There", so I sang it quietly to myself with my arms around my sister and brother. Finally, I couldn't stand it any more, being in there day and night, listening to the wailing. The people were kind to us and gave us something to eat, but I was worried about my mother and father—I couldn't see what was happening to them. I didn't know if there was a God or not—my parents had said there wasn't any God. But just in case there was one, I said a little prayer to God to please keep my mother and father safe. When my mother came to see us between air raids, I told her we were going back with her because I couldn't stand it here with all the praying out loud—it was scaring me. So she took us back to our own shelter with her, and there we stayed. One day the machine gun nest was gone. The Japanese soldiers had left without our knowing when they did.

Now at night there was a deep red glow in the sky to the northwest, much redder than any sunset. The red glow changed to high red flames that lit up the whole sky. It would have been beautiful to see if it had not been so terrible. We knew what it was—Manila was burning. The Japanese knew they were losing the war so they started burning the city, unlike General MacArthur who had surrendered the city rather than see it destroyed. My father was afraid for all his papers in the Bureau of Science. He had been working there during the Japanese occupation, continuing his studies of population. When the bombing started, he had no time to bring his papers home. He wanted to go into Manila and try to save his papers but my mother begged him not to—it was too dangerous. *After the war, he went back to the Bureau of Science and found nothing left of his papers. Everything he had worked on all his life had been burned.*

The Japanese also burned the towns around Manila, including San Juan, the town nearest us. We could hear machine gun and rifle fire coming from nearby but, suddenly, the Japanese and Korean soldiers disappeared from our neighborhood. We knew the war was almost over and we could sing out loud.

I ran after every U.S. Army jeep or truck that came down our road, yelling "Hello Joe! Chocolate Joe!"

14

Hello Joe! Chocolate, Joe!

It was a glorious day in 1945 when the U.S. Army's lst Cavalry roared into our neighborhood in huge tanks and trucks. We knew they were coming because gunfire and strafing by American airplanes around us had been nonstop for several days. People said the Americans had liberated the town of San Juan; they were shooting their way into our foothills along with the guerrillas who had come out of the mountains to join them.

Some days before, all the Japanese and Koreans had suddenly left our neighborhood. When that happened, there was pandemonium. The people ran into the vegetable fields that the Koreans had guarded and ripped up all the vegetables to take home. A big storehouse where the Japanese had kept sacks and sacks of rice was torn open, and people were crushing in to take away as much rice as they could. In the Philippines, rice is the most important food, and no one had had hardly any rice for a long time.

I was overcome with excitement. My parents told us to stay indoors, although there was only sporadic gunfire. I couldn't understand why my father wasn't running out to the warehouse to get rice as everyone else was doing.

"Daddy, let's go and get some rice!" I was running back and forth from the front porch to his chair. He walked with me to the front door to watch the people running along the road. He said, "The worse thing you could ever do is to take anything that does not belong to you. The rice does not belong to us. Those people are looting." I was suddenly subdued. I couldn't understand— if it was wrong to take the rice, why were all our neighbors doing it?

It wasn't always easy to know what was right or what was wrong. Once, I was in a neighbor's house and walked into their dining room. No one else was in the room, and there on the dining room table was a bowl of bananas. I was very hungry, went up to the table, pulled a banana quickly off the bunch, and put it in my pocket. Later outside, I peeled it and ate it fast, hoping no one had seen me. All the rest of the day, I didn't feel very good. I knew I shouldn't have done what I did. Why did I do it? That night, I couldn't get to sleep for a long time. I wanted to tell someone about what I had done.

The next morning, when no one else was around, I told my mother about it. I was crying. She put her arms around me and said, "If someone had some bananas and didn't offer one to a starving little girl, they deserve to have that banana taken! You didn't do anything wrong. But don't tell your father about this." I nodded through my tears.

My crying finally stopped, but I still didn't feel good. I knew it was wrong to take the banana. Why did my mother not say so? I knew that my father would say it was wrong, and he would be very angry at me. That was why my mother didn't want him to know—she didn't want him to get angry. I also realized that my mother truly did not believe that what I did was wrong. But my father

*would have. Which of them was right? I knew, then, that
I could never ask anyone else about right and wrong—
from then on, I had to decide for myself.*

The roar of the American tanks and trucks coming
up our road was one of the most exciting sounds I have
ever heard. All the people, including us, stood along the
roads, waving and shouting and screaming, "Hello, Joe!"
and "Cigarette, Joe!" and "Chocolate, Joe!" Behind the
tanks came huge brown trucks with no roofs, filled with
U.S. Army soldiers carrying rifles, waving and grinning
at us, and throwing cigarette packs and other things to
the people jumping up and down along the road. Dust
was everywhere, but no one cared.

Something fell in the road in front of me, thrown by
a grinning American soldier. I picked it up quickly. It
was something wrapped in paper, with brown writing
that said "Hershey." My mother, standing next to me,
said "Open it, Pooh, it is a chocolate bar!" And so it
was. It was not like the Hershey bars around today. It
was narrower—about one inch wide, about two-to-three
inches long, and about one inch thick, and divided into
three equal sections. It was part of the army's "D" ra-
tions, I later found out. My first D-ration Hershey bar,
and the taste of it on my tongue is something I have
never forgotten. Nothing else in this world has a taste
and feeling compared to that.

From then on, I ran after every U.S. Army jeep or
truck that came down our road, yelling "Hello, Joe!
Chocolate, Joe!" Sometimes I'd get one, sometimes not.
I also yelled for cigarettes because I remembered that
my mother liked to smoke. She liked Camels and Lucky
Strike. My father smoked the cigarettes, too, but he
preferred his pipe. He would tear open the cigarette
paper and stuff the cigarette tobacco into the bowl of
his pipe.

After that day, there was one excitement after another. The lst Cavalry set up camp in the fields about a half-mile from our house. We kids in the neighborhood would spend every chance we got in the camps. I was at a decided advantage, being able to speak English. My mother had never learned more than a few words of the native dialect, *Tagalog*, so we always spoke English at home. Outside my home, I spoke the dialect. Sometimes, when I couldn't quickly think of the right word in one language, I'd use a word from the other language, almost without knowing what I was doing. If my father heard this, he would stop it. He insisted that we not mix up the two languages in the same sentence or even in the same conversation. He said if we couldn't think of the right word in one language, it was just laziness.

I got my first taste of Coca Cola in the U.S. Army camp—there was a big barrel of it propped up above the ground and the barrel had a spigot. One soldier gave me a metal canteen and he showed me how to open the spigot and get a thick black syrup into my canteen. He told me not to take too much of the syrup, just a little, and then fill the canteen up the rest of the way with water. It was delicious. It didn't have the fizz that Coca Cola from a bottle had, and it was warm from sitting in the sun and being in my canteen all day, but it was delicious. Sometimes I wouldn't add any water at all, but drink the syrup straight. It was better with water.

Another camp was set up for sick soldiers. It was surrounded by barbed wire, and no one was allowed in that camp. However, we were allowed to come to the movies shown in that camp some nights. The big movie screen was set up outdoors, about 20 feet on the outside of the barbed wire fence. All the soldiers, most of whom were wearing light blue hospital pajamas, sat inside the fence on benches facing the screen. The neigh-

borhood people sat outside the fence, on the ground between the fence and the screen. Whenever my parents
let me go (which was about one night a week), I would
get there before the sun went down to pick a best spot.
As soon as it got dark enough, the show would begin. It always began with singing. Not many of the soldiers would be on their benches for the singing, but one
by one the benches filled up. The words of the song were
put on the screen, and there was a ball on the screen
that bounced from word to word in time to the song
being sung over the loudspeakers. I learned many American songs that way. The ones I liked best were "You
Are My Sunshine" and "Mairsy Doats". The "Sunshine"
song went like this:

You are my sunshine, my only sunshine,
You make me happy when skies are gray,
You'll never know, dear, how much I love you—
Please don't take my sunshine away.

The other night, dear, while I lay sleeping
I dreamt I held you in my arms,
But when I woke up, I was mistaken –
Please don't take my sunshine away.

You are my sunshine, my only sunshine,
You make me happy when skies are gray,
You'll never know, dear, how much I love you –
Please don't take my sunshine away.

I would sing at the top of my lungs. The soldiers'
voices would be the loudest of all. The people from the
neighborhood wouldn't sing—they were impatient for
the movie to begin. But I loved the singing and was always sorry when it ended, although I, too, was eager

for the movie to begin. My father never came to the movies, nor did he want my mother to go. But once in a while she did. My mother loved to sing, too. Her favorite song during those evening sing-alongs was "Don't Fence Me In."

Some of the soldiers in the camp would ask about my family. They wanted to know why I spoke English so well and didn't look "very Filipino." I explained to them that my father was Filipino and my mother was Irish who grew up in America, in Tracy, California. They wanted to meet my mother, so I invited them to come to my house. My parents were always glad to see the soldiers. When my mother wasn't feeling too sick, she would cook fried chicken for them. We kept some native chickens in our chicken coop for eggs and hatching chicks.

The soldiers liked coming to our house to visit and eat fried chicken. Sometimes, my mother would make chicken fricassee and dumplings for a change. The soldiers would always bring cans of C-rations, fruit cocktail, and cigarettes for my parents. They would sit at our round black table, covered with my mother's lace tablecloth, listen to my father talk, and eat my mother's fried chicken. During those exciting days, going to the well to keep our water drum full and doing all my other jobs around the house, made me impatient—I would much rather stay in the camps, talk to the soldiers, and read their comic books.

Comic books were a subject of argument between my parents and me—I was not allowed to read them. Before the war my father had read to us some of the comics in the Sunday newspaper. He especially liked the Katzenjammer Kids. After the war, comic books like Superman, Donald Duck, Archie, and Captain Marvel came into our neighborhood from the U.S. Army camps. At the corner store the Chinese storekeeper, Mang Gorio

(Mr. Gorio), had a rack of comic books outside that were not for sale but could be rented. The top racks had the almost-new comic books that rented for 10 centavos, the middle racks had older comic books for 5 centavos, and the bottom racks had really old comic books, most of which no longer had covers. These could be rented for 2 centavos (a centavo is similar to a penny). We kids in the neighborhood would periodically check the racks as we ran by the store to see whether the Superman comics had made its way down the racks. We could never figure out how Mang Gorio decided when to move a comic book from the 10 centavo rack to the 5 centavo rack, or down to the 2 centavo rack.

If you wanted to rent a comic book, you paid Mang Gorio your money, picked out a comic book from the rack, and sat down on one of the big stones by the road-side to read it. Often, there were two or three kids look-ing at the same comic book. Mang Gorio did not object to this—he knew that many kids did not have even one centavo. He had a rule, though, that you couldn't pass a comic book from one kid to another. You had to read it together. None of us had ever heard him say this rule but somehow we knew it. Most of the kids could not read English but figured out the story from the pictures.

Inside Mang Gorio's store were brand-new comic books for sale. I didn't have money to rent a comic book very often, and certainly never enough to buy one, but once in a while if Mang Gorio was in a good mood, he would let me read a brand-new comic book for free, just before he would hang it on his for-rent rack. The first thing I did was to open up the comic book and hold it to my face—I loved the smell of a brand new comic book. But I was always careful not to bend or wrinkle it. I never asked Mang Gorio to let me read a comic book— sometimes, when I would be at his store buying vinegar

*or candles or something, he would nod his head at me
and hand me a new comic book. I never saw him do this
with the other kids, and he never did it when any other
kid was around. I think he liked me because I didn't call
him names or throw stones at the wall of his store as
some kids did.*

*My parents would have been angry if they knew that
I rented, or read, comics. One day I complained to my
mother, asking her why other kids could read comics
but I wasn't allowed to. She said comic books were "brain
burners." What this meant was that if you read too many
of them, your brain would become useless for anything
else – all you would want to do was read comic books.
This didn't sound very possible to me; I didn't see anything wrong in reading comic books and I said so. But I
didn't say I was reading Mang Gorio's.*

*One evening my mother came home with a paper
bag and handed it to me. Inside were two comic books.
I pulled them out. They were brand new, crisp and
smelling wonderfully. But I had never seen this kind
before. They were both "Classic Comics", stories from
books that I had already read. I liked them but they
weren't the same as Superman or Captain Marvel, my
favorites. Another night she came home with a "True
Comics" about Joe Louis, a champion boxer in
America; people called him the "Brown Bomber". He
was a real man who was still alive. I liked that comic
book, and read it over and over; I particularly liked
the part where he knocked out Max Schmeling when
no one thought he could win. My father said that even
these comic books were "brain burners" but he let me
keep them because my mother had brought them. She
didn't bring any more home, however, and I continued
to read Mang Gorio's comic books and those in the U.S.
Army camps.*

The American soldiers loved fried chicken. The people in the neighborhood invited some of the soldiers to their houses for fried chicken once in a while. I guess this gave one of our Chinese neighbors, Mr. Wong, the idea of opening a restaurant serving fried chicken and other dishes. Mr. Wong took over an old burned out two-storied building filled with broken concrete and tall weeds. The neighborhood kids used to play in that building because it had concrete beams high above the ground. We would climb up to one of the beams and walk across it, balancing carefully. It was scary and we would not let the little kids do it. My sister would threaten to tell my parents but she never did because she knew that I'd get mad at her and wouldn't take her with me when I'd go places.

When Mr. Wong fixed the burned building, we could no longer play there. He also built a fence with the words *"BAWAL PUMASOK"* ("NO TRESPASSING") painted on a sign. Mr. Wong hung pretty colored lanterns around the yard, and set out chairs and tables at which food was served. He put up a big sign on the house that said "Wong's Garden. Chinese and American Dishes." Every evening, American soldiers came to have supper. Sometimes, they had older girls from the neighborhood with them and whenever we kids would peer through the fence of Mr. Wong's Garden, the girls and the soldiers eating at the tables were always laughing and having a good time.

One day, after the 1st Cavalry had left our neighborhood and had been replaced by the 37th Infantry, one of my soldier friends came to our house for supper, bringing another soldier with him. During the conversation with my parents, it turned out that this soldier was one of the grown children of a woman in Canada who had married my grandfather. She was his third wife. He said his stepfather (my grandfather) had said he had a daughter living in the Philippines but had lost touch with her and didn't know what had become of her during the war. My mother began to cry. The soldier had us all stand outside in the front yard and took a snapshot of us with his camera. He was very excited about writing to his stepfather and sending him a picture of us. My mother wrote a letter to my grandfather, too, for the soldier to include in his letter. That snapshot and letter were eventually to bring us to America, but we did not know it then. In the meantime, I would go through the best time, and the worst time, of my 12 years.

15

Cherry Pie

The biggest attraction of the U.S. Army camps in our neighborhood was food. One camp set up its field kitchen in a rented house that had a very big back yard, surrounded by a high wire fence. At breakfast, lunch, and supper, the soldiers in the camp would file into the yard and line up in front of big, steaming pots of food, and a table loaded with bread and pies. An Army sergeant and his helpers would ladle out the food onto the metal mess kits held out by the soldiers. The soldiers would take their mess kits of food and sit around under the trees in the yard. We, the neighborhood children, pressed against the outside of the fence, clutching tin cans with make-shift wire handles. We would start congregating at the fence long before meals were served, waiting and watching the soldiers eat.

At the end of the meal, the soldiers would rinse out their kits at a faucet and file out of the yard. That would be a signal for us kids to begin shoving and jostling, climbing the fence and reaching over it with our tin cans. The sergeant's helpers would take our cans, one by one, and fill them with food left over in the pots. We were always on the lookout for special treats, such as cherry pie. It would not matter that the pieces of pie were lumped on top of potatoes and gravy, or stew, in our cans. There was never enough cherry pie for every can. The biggest boys got their cans over the fence first, and usually got the cherry pie. I wasn't very big and would hardly ever get cherry pie in my can. After our cans were handed back over the fence, we would disperse into the neighborhood, taking the precious food back to our homes for our families next meal.

One morning, nose to the fence with the other kids as usual, waiting for breakfast to be over, I noticed that behind the steaming pots several soldiers were standing near some tables peeling potatoes for the noon meal. I had an idea. I could get a job in that field kitchen peeling potatoes. I dashed home with my can of scrambled eggs, combed my hair with water, put on a clean shirt and ran back to the field kitchen. Only a few soldiers were working in the kitchen area. I went up to the sergeant, a very big soldier wearing his olive-drab uniform pants, boots, T-shirt, and cap. I asked him if I could work in his kitchen; he wouldn't have to pay me money, just let me have some left-over food. He looked down at me, his hands on his hips. He seemed surprised that I could speak such good English.

"What kind of work can you do?" he asked me.

"I can peel potatoes," I answered. I had never peeled a potato in my life, but I had watched the soldiers do it, I had seen cartoon pictures of Private Dave Breger doing it, and I had peeled camotes. I was sure I could peel potatoes.

"How old are you?" he asked.

"Eleven," I answered.

"You look small for eleven," he said.

"I'm strong, and I never get sick," I said.

He thought for a minute, and then said, "O.K. You

can start by washing out those pots." He pointed to a pile of big metal pots beside the yard faucet.

I began to work. I was in seventh heaven. I was doing real work, and I was going to get paid. All day was bliss. The sergeant's helpers all talked to me, they showed me pictures of their families. I peeled potatoes and chopped onions, tears streaming down my face from the onions and sniffling until one of the soldiers gave me his olive-drab handkerchief to blow my nose. He told me to keep the handkerchief and I did—for years. At lunch time, I was all puffed up with pride as I helped ladle out the food to the soldiers, while the neighborhood kids at the fence stared at me in silence (also envy, I suspected). After the soldiers had their lunch, and the leftovers had been distributed to the kids at the fence, I sat down with the sergeant and his helpers under the trees and had lunch myself. There was no cherry pie that day, but it didn't matter to me at all. I was totally happy.

After lunch we cleaned up, and the sergeant and his helpers left for a rest. I stayed around the yard, cleaning everything up better. Then it was time to prepare the evening meal, and all was busy again. The supper routine went much the same as lunch, except that there were more kinds of food. The sergeant told me to save out all the food I needed to take home to my family before the soldiers filed in. He gave me several cans to put the food in so that they wouldn't be all mashed up together. He also gave me a big cardboard box for carrying home all the cans of food, and an unopened box of Milky Way candy bars!

After supper, it was getting dark but there was still cleaning up to do. While I was finishing the cleaning, I saw my mother come through the gate. When I hadn't come home all day, she had started looking for me and one of the neighborhood kids told her where I was. I

ran to her, saying excitedly, "Mommy, I have a job!" The
sergeant saw her and came over to us.

"Ma'am," he said, "is this your little girl?"

"Yes," my mother answered.

"Please, ma'am, take her home. If the captain finds
out that I have a female in my kitchen. . . ." He shook
his head, not finishing his sentence. I listened with a
sinking feeling in the pit of my stomach.

"Why didn't you tell her yourself?" my mother asked
him.

"Ma'am, when she looked at me with those big eyes
of hers and asked for a job, I couldn't say no. Please
take her home."

I didn't wait to see how the conversation ended, or
notice that the sergeant had given my mother the box
of food to take home. I ran out of that field kitchen and
all the way home in the dark, tears stinging my eyes. I
was disappointed, but I was also angry. I think I was
more angry than anything else. *It wasn't fair! Why
should it matter that I was a girl? I could do the work
even better than a boy could! Why couldn't I have been
born a boy?*

When I got home, my father was waiting for me,
furious that I had been gone all day without telling
anyone where I was, and getting home after dark. He
was still lecturing to me when my mother got back with
the box of food. I didn't think it would be any use to
explain anything to him. My mother did, later. Also
later, she told me that the sergeant was sorry he
couldn't let me work in his kitchen anymore, and he
said that I had been a very good worker. She also said
he was inviting me to have supper with him and the
soldiers in his kitchen the next evening, when they
would be having cherry pie. I did not go, nor did I ever
return to the fence with my can. I went to another

fence, in another camp, with another field kitchen, although it was much farther from my house. I found out later from the other kids that one of the older boys from the neighborhood, one of my worst enemies, was working as a helper in the sergeant's kitchen. That made me more angry. I didn't stay angry very long, however, because something else came into my life—a Piper Cub.

My airplane and I dropped straight down, landing
with a shattering crash.

16

Lieutenant George Intile

From the time I was six years old, I had been fascinated by flight. My mother had given me a book, at
Christmas of 1940, called "How They Blazed the Way—
Men Who Have Advanced Civilization," by J. Walker
McSpadden. The book contained biographies of important people, starting with Hippocrates and ending with
Wilber and Orville Wright, and including Madame Curie. My favorites were Leonardo Da Vinci, Thomas
Edison, Madame Curie, and the Wright brothers. After
finishing the book (which I re-read many times over), I
decided to become an inventor—and to fly. Once, when
I was about seven years old, I took a big umbrella,
opened it up and jumped from a small balcony of our
two-story house in Manila. I had visions of myself float-
ing gently to the ground, like the Montgolfier brothers
and their gas-filled balloon. I was rudely shocked by hitting the ground very hard, with the breath knocked out
of me. The umbrella was broken but I wasn't—just frightened at not being able to breathe as I lay there. This
may have been one reason that my parents often told
me that I had no common sense. I didn't know quite what
they meant—I usually thought out, ahead, what I was

going to do, but somehow, things never turned out to be as I had planned.

Another time, when I was about nine years old, and we had moved to the house in the hills of San Juan, I built an "airplane" out of a wooden crate, with wood slabs and pieces nailed together, and set it right at the edge of the hill near our house. I got into it and instructed my little brother, Trotsky, who was about four years old, to give my airplane a shove to launch it.

"Push it," I said. I knew, of course, that without an engine and propeller my "airplane" would not fly, but I was sure it would gently glide through the air and land gracefully at the bottom of the hill. My brother was not so sure.

"No," he said.

"PUSH IT," I said sternly. So Trotsky, who was used to obeying me, pushed it. My airplane and I dropped straight down, landing with a shattering crash, the box breaking apart and the wings thrown off, hitting me on the head. I sat there on the ground, amid the remnants of my airplane, with my pride completely wounded and my brother staring silently at me from the top of the hill, his thumb in his mouth. I was more frustrated than hurt when I finally stood up, although my back, bottom, and head continued to hurt for a couple of days. I couldn't understand why my airplane did not glide as it had been intended to do.

When the U.S. 1st Cavalry roared into our neighborhood, they were accompanied by army observation planes. A small landing strip was set up in a flat area of the fields about a mile from our house, and these little observation planes would take off for parts unknown, then return to land. I watched for them wherever I was, and if I was inside the house and heard the engines in the distance, I would run outside to look for them. Whenever my parents let me (and sometimes when they didn't know about it), I would go to the landing field and sit on the grass outside the barbed wire fence around it and watch the airplanes take off and land. They were small, single-engine aircraft—"Piper Cubs" they were called, I found out later.

One evening, my sister and I were playing "kick the can" with some other kids in the road in front of our house. There were several variations of this game. In one variation, a tin can was set up in the middle of the road and a line drawn in the road about 15 feet from the can. One kid was "It" and stood by the side of the road. The main objective of the game was for the rest of us to stand at the line and each try to knock the can over with a stone, run to pick up that stone, and run back to the line before the "It" could set the can back up and try to tag you. If you weren't fast enough and were tagged, you would be the next "It." Or, you could push your stone over one foot using the other foot (but no hands) and try to walk back to the line balancing the stone on your foot. The "It" couldn't tag you as long as the stone was on your foot. If the stone fell off your foot before you got back across the line, the "It" could tag you.

"Kick-the-can" was a great game to play in the evenings, especially on moonlit nights. It also allowed for lots of *saling pusa*. The little ones could throw stones at the can (mostly never hitting it) and run back and forth to their heart's content. To give them a thrill, the "It" would pretend to try and tag them and they would run screaming with excitement across the line. Almost every older kid had a younger sister or brother to take care of. If you wanted to go play somewhere, you had to take the little one with you. None of us thought to complain—this was just the way it was. If the little one was a baby, you set him or her down alongside the road with some stones to play with. You didn't have to change any diapers because none of the babies wore any. If the baby screamed while you were playing, you had to pick it up and carry it while you played. Everything was easier if the little one was old enough to be "*saling pusa.*"

On the evening I am describing, it had not yet gotten dark. Our game was in full noise when two American soldiers came down the road. We stopped to let them pass, but they stayed to watch our game. One was a captain and the other a 1st lieutenant. I could tell by the silver bars on their uniforms and caps—1st lieutenants had one silver bar, 2nd lieutenants had one gold bar and captains had two silver bars attached together. 1st lieutenants were higher rank than 2nd lieutenants, and captains were higher rank than 1st lieutenants.

I left the game to go over and talk to the officers and explain the game to them. My sister was beside me. The officers were surprised at my English and asked me my name. I said my name was Barbara Ann, and my sister's name was Snuffy. The captain seemed startled. He said he was Captain Singleton, and the other officer was Lieutenant Intile. Captain Singleton said he had two daughters about our age and their names were Barbara Ann and Snuffy! They wanted to meet our parents who were sitting on the porch of our house. We went up to the porch steps, and the officers introduced themselves to my parents. They said they were pilots of the army observation airplanes that were stationed at the little airstrip in our neighborhood. I was enthralled. I couldn't stop asking them about their airplanes.

Captain Singleton and Lieutenant Intile became good friends of our family. They would come for supper sometimes and always brought canned goods. They would fly over our house and wig-wag the wings of their airplanes if they saw me outside. I could never tell which one it was but I would always jump up and down and wave. Lieutenant Intile's first name was George and he must have been around 23 years old. He had a sister in New Jersey named Karen who was a few years older than I was; Karen and I wrote a few letters to each other. She sent me a dark blue wool skirt in the mail to Lieutenant Intile. The best part was when Lieutenant Intile said he would teach me all the parts of his airplane and, when I had learned all the parts, he would teach me to fly it. My wildest dream was coming true!

I don't remember how long it took me to learn all the parts of Lieutenant Intile's airplane. One part I kept forgetting was the jury strut, a small piece attached to the wings. I learned about the ailerons and how they worked, how the rudder, elevator, and stabilizer worked. I learned about all the dials inside the cockpit and what they indicated. When Lieutenant Intile had no time for me, I would continue to sit outside the barbed wire fence and watch the airplanes take off and land.

Lieutenant Intile also taught me how to recognize the different Army airplanes that flew overhead, not only from how they looked but from how they sounded. Sometimes, when we would hear an airplane in the distance he would test me. He loaned me some of his "Flying" magazines where there were pictures of airplanes I had never seen. He told me that the "Spitfire" and the "Mustang" were the best fighter planes in the world. I read almost everything in the "Flying" magazines, and secretly wished that I could be a test pilot when I grew up.

One day, Lieutenant Intile said I had learned all there was to learn about his airplane, and although he had said he would teach me to fly it, he was sorry but army regulations would not allow civilians to be taken into the air. However, he would let me taxi the plane along the ground. I was as excited as I could possibly be; it didn't matter that I would not be able to go into the air. Lieutenant Intile had taught me how to control the throttle and how to yell "CONTACT" after he had cranked the propeller a few times. Also, I knew what NOT to do. He shut the door of the airplane (but did not latch it) and I was on my own. He cranked the propeller, I pushed the throttle yelling "CONTACT," the engine roared and I was rolling down the runway. He pointed to where I was supposed to stop, and I stopped and turned off the engine. He came up to the door of the cockpit, grinning. There was never a more intoxicated 11-year old girl in the entire world, I am convinced.

Some days later, while I was reading one of the "Flying" magazines, I came across an advertisement for a pamphlet called "How to Fly a Piper Cub." My father let me have some money to send to Karen with the order blank, and she must have mailed it to the company because, many months later, the pamphlet came in our mailbox for me. I knew most of the things in the pamphlet already, because of what I had learned from Lieutenant Intile, but I read that little pamphlet over and over. I still have it.

Then one day, Captain Singleton and Lieutenant Intile came to say goodbye. The lst Cavalry was leaving our neighborhood. Some time later we got a letter from them. They were in Japan, and Captain Singleton had been promoted to major. I was sorry that Lieutenant Intile had already gone when my Piper Cub pamphlet arrived—there was no one to show it to.

Although the little airstrip was dismantled when the lst Cavalry left, there was still an airfield I could get to, a much bigger one, with C-47s and larger aircraft like the B-24 bomber. There were also Mustang fighters.

The big airfield was called Camp Murphy, and it was about 10 or 12 miles from our house. I knew a shortcut, across fields and brushland, but it was still a very long way so I didn't go there very often.

One day, my friend Carmelita and I, and my little brother, started off early in the morning for Camp Murphy. My mother said I could go if I took Trotsky with us; he wanted to see the airplanes, too. Carmelita's father said she could go if she collected firewood and brought it back. It was very hard to find firewood around our neighborhood because all the firewood had been used up. We had to go farther and farther away to find firewood. At our house, we used a sawdust stove, made from two tin cans, for cooking. I collected the sawdust from a sawmill that had just opened up in the town of Mandaluyong. We also used pieces of an old wood telephone pole for our cooking fire. The only trouble with this wood was that it was impregnated with creosote so that the wood wouldn't be eaten up by termites while it was a telephone pole. Whenever we cooked with this wood, some of the soot from the burning creosote got onto everything. The walls of our house were black with the soot, and we kids always looked grimy. Even the little brown house lizards that scurried along our ceilings and laid their eggs in our bookcases, were gray from the soot.

When Carmelita, Trotsky, and I started out, it was a beautiful day. I brought my canteen filled with water, strapped around my waist, and some food. I knew I would have to carry my brother on my back every now and then—it was a very long way to walk, and he wasn't very strong because he was often sick.

We got to the edge of the airfield around noon, sat down in the shade of a tree and ate our lunch, watching the airplanes take off and land. We covered our ears sometimes because they hurt from the roar of the engines. We couldn't stay too long because we had a long walk back, and Carmelita still had to collect firewood. We had seen quite a bit of firewood on our way to the airfield so we knew we would be able to collect all she could carry. She tied the huge bundle with a strip of cloth and balanced it on her head with one hand.

It took us longer to collect the firewood than we had expected. I guess we were a little tired and were walking slower. I was carrying my brother now all the way on my back because he was very tired. Just as the sun was setting, we suddenly heard rifle shots very close, and bullets whistled past our ears as we trudged through a small clump of trees. I dumped my brother on the ground and lay on top of him. I didn't want any bullets to hit him. Carmelita was also lying on the ground. We crawled on our bellies over to a fallen log nearby and huddled against it, close to each other, being as quiet as we could. Some more shots were fired and the bullets sent the dust spurting around us. Trotsky was very brave and made no sound. Carmelita started to cry a little, but she covered her own mouth with her hand. We lay there for a long time it seemed, after those last shots were fired. It had gotten dark so I whispered that we should start crawling away from there. As we started, I noticed that Carmelita was dragging her bundle of firewood behind her. I told her to leave the wood but she wouldn't. She whispered that her father would be very angry if she came home without firewood. So she dragged her firewood as we crawled away until we got some distance. There were no more shots and since it had gotten dark, I said, "Let's stand up and run!"

I put my brother on my back so we could move faster. Carmelita, however, insisted on carrying that huge long bundle of firewood on her head and couldn't run very fast. I said I'd help, so she took one end of the bundle and I took the other end. I told my brother to hold on to my neck as tight as he could because I had only one arm behind me to support him. We ran as fast as we could until we reached the outskirts of our neighborhood. We were panting very hard, we were very tired, and we were very, very relieved. We went first to Carmelita's house where she took the firewood in. I got home with Trotsky to find my mother worried because we were so late. I explained what had happened, and she insisted I go to the army camp and report the sniper to the soldiers. (A "sniper" is someone you can't see, who shoots at you from a hiding place). I did, they immediately got a jeep, and I guided them to the area. I pointed out the trees where I had thought the rifle fire had come from, and I stayed in the jeep while the soldiers investigated. It was very quiet while I waited there in the dark, except for the sound of the soldiers in the distance. They didn't find anything except empty rifle shells.

Later, Carmelita said that her father had not scolded her for coming home late because of all the firewood she had brought. My parents were not mad at me, either, but they said I could not go to the Camp Murphy airfield again. Instead, my father said, he would take me to visit my cousin.

Bamboo rod

Packed sawdust

large tin can

small tin can

kindling   Stove, with cooking pot

Sawdust Cooking Stove—the sawdust is packed very firmly around the bamboo rod held upright in the center of the large can (about 2 gallons in size). The rod is then very carefully pulled out, leaving a center hole for air in the packed sawdust. Paper and twigs are slipped into the bottom of the can through the small tin can (about the size of an evaporated milk can), and the kindling is lit with a match. Soon the burning kindling sets fire to the sawdust, which burns slowly and lasts for an hour or two. The cooking pot sits on top of the whole stove. This stove is best for cooking rice and for simmering slowly. It is not good for cooking things quickly.

17

The Psychopathic Hospital

My father found out that one of his nephews, Enrique (this is not his real name), was in the Psychopathic Hospital. I remembered him as a very fat young man who had come to our house several times before the war when I was about six years old. He made my sister and I laugh because he would sit in our little rocker and then stand up. The rocker would stick to his rear end, and he would walk around the living room, bent over, with the rocker stuck. He also brought us candy. He was our favorite cousin and, in fact, the only cousin we knew because the others were in the Visayan Islands and were grown up.

My father announced that he was going to visit Enrique and would take me with him. I wanted to see my cousin again, but my mother said no. I listened to my parents argue.

"Phil," my mother said, "she is too young to go there."

"She is going to have to learn sometime, and it might as well be now," said my father. He wanted me to learn about everything. So I went with him.

The trip by caretella and jitney was long and dusty. Along the way my father explained that the Psychopathic Hospital was not like the other kind of hospitals I had seen; this was a hospital for people who had sickness in their minds, not in their bodies. I asked him what sickness in the mind did Enrique have. My father said he didn't know, which was one reason he wanted to visit him.

The hospital buildings were very large. Inside, there was a bad smell and I could hear faint screams. I began to feel uneasy because of the screams, which grew louder and louder as we followed our guide along the dark hallways. The ends of the hallways were closed by doors made of iron bars; the doors were unlocked and locked each time by our guide. Finally, we stepped into a huge room divided up into smaller compartments, each surrounded by bars. Now I could see where the screams were coming from. The compartments had men in them. Some of the men were crouching in corners, some were trying to climb up the bars, some were screaming, and some were naked. I moved closer to my father as we followed our guide.

"Don't be afraid," my father said. "These people won't hurt you; they are only sick." But I wasn't thinking about them hurting me, I just didn't like to hear the screaming. It was the screaming that frightened me.

Our guide unlocked a compartment, let us in, and then locked it again. I saw Enrique; he was squatting on the floor and wearing white pajamas. There were no beds or chairs in the compartment, just Enrique. He was very thin, not fat as I had remembered. He saw us and stood up. My father went to him and put his arms around him. Enrique was happy to see us. He and my father began talking and they seemed to forget that I was there. I stood still, hearing the screams of the men in the other compartments. I did not want to look at them; I stared down at the wet concrete floor. It looked as though the floor had just been hosed down with water. After a while, my father said we had to go. I shook hands with Enrique, and he told us to come again. He wanted my father to come live with him here, and he showed my father the hole in the floor which was used as the toilet. My father nodded his head, saying, yes, he could come live here but it would be better if Enrique could come and live with us. I certainly agreed with my father, but did not say anything.

That evening, when my father was sitting in the wicker rocker on our front porch, silently smoking his pipe, I asked him what he was thinking about. He said, "I'm thinking about what it would be like to live with Enrique in the Psychopathic Hospital. It would be interesting to study the people while I was living there."

"Are you going to live there, Daddy?" I was worried.

"Of course not," he said. "I was just thinking about it." Sometimes, I, too, would think about what it would be like to live there. I was sure I didn't want to. Sometime later, Enrique did leave the hospital. He came to see us before he went back to the Visayan Islands. He was not so thin anymore, and he and my father talked a long time on the front porch before he left.

18

Heroes on the Front Porch

Our front porch wasn't very big—there was just enough room for a white wicker arm chair on one side of the front door and a white wicker rocker on the other side of the door. Three wooden steps led down from the porch to the walkway that went to the front gate. The walkway was narrow and once had flagstones, but many were missing and others were broken. Weeds grew up between the broken stones, and I could always find crickets among those weeds. *Kalachuchi* trees grew on each side of the front gate; these trees were really very large plants, but the branches and stems were smooth and thick enough to climb upon. You had to be very careful to step only between the forks of the branches because the branches were very brittle and could snap off quickly, oozing a white sap at the break. These plant-trees were covered in white flowers with yellowish centers; kalachuchi flowers have a very strong fragrance that can be smelled from far away.

Between the kalachuchi trees was a wooden gate with slats missing. The gate was quite broken down, but my father insisted that we open and shut the front gate instead of stepping through it. That gate was a standing joke in our family, except it wasn't a joke to my father. He would spend time fixing the rusty gate hinges with old wire; the hinges had lost most of their screws and were attached to rotting wood posts. (In tropical countries, wood rots very quickly because of termites and the weather). Whenever we opened or shut the front gate we would giggle because anyone could step right through it; sometimes, the gate would fall right over.

Once, in exasperation, when I had to run back because I had forgotten to "shut the gate," I asked my father why the gate had to be shut when anyone could just step right through it or push it over. He said it was the principle of the thing. *The Principle Of The Thing— that was a phrase I heard quite often from him; it was his standard answer whenever I had a complaint about something that I thought was unreasonable. It was never a satisfying response as far as I was concerned but over the years I got used to it and eventually began to understand what it meant. In the case of the front gate, it seemed to mean that the purpose of the gate was not to keep people out but to let them know that this was our house and our yard, not part of the road or even part of the rest of the world. The front gate was a sign that this was our place.*

After people came through the gate, everyone liked to sit on the front porch. If the two wicker chairs were occupied, we sat on the steps. A wooden railing went around most of the porch, but it was wobbly and would have fallen over if anyone sat on it. My father's study filled up most of the living room, so the front porch was usually our sitting room for the few people who came to visit. We hardly ever had any visitors except for the American soldiers who always sat at our dining room table to eat and talk.

One day, soon after the war had ended, we had two exciting visitors who were not American soldiers. They

were Colonel Marking and his wife, Yay. Colonel Marking, whose real name was Marcus Agustin, was the
leader of Marking's Guerrillas who had caused so much
trouble for the Japanese Army by their sabotage activities. Yay had joined Marking's band of guerrillas and
had stayed with him in the mountains for most of the
war. I saw Colonel Marking and Yay as heroes.

By that time, I already had several heroes—
Leonardo da Vinci, Thomas Edison, Madame Curie,
Wilbur and Orville Wright. I also had a favorite Philippine national hero, Jose Rizal. He had been a medical
doctor and writer who lived between 1861 and 1896.
Through novels and other writings, he raised the hopes
and fighting spirit of the Filipino people who were under oppression and tyranny by Spain. He constantly
aroused the anger of the Spanish authorities, who eventually had him executed by a firing squad when he was
only 35 years old. The site of that execution, a field called
Bagumbayan, is now marked by a memorial to Dr. Rizal
and is part of a large park, the *Luneta* (now called Rizal
Park), along the shore of Manila Bay. The night before
he was shot, Rizal wrote a long poem and hid it in a
lamp in his prison cell. The poem was found later by his
brother. Written in Spanish, the poem was titled *"Mi
Ultimo Adios"* (*"My Last Farewell"*), and it was his
goodbye to our country. It always made me feel like crying when I read it. Here is an English translation of the
first stanza:

Fare thee well, motherland that I adore, region the sun holds dear,
Pearl of the sea oriental, our paradise come to grief;
I go with gladness to give thee my life all withered and drear;
Though it were more brilliant, more fresh with flowery cheer,
Even then for thee would I give it, would give it for thy relief.

Among all the people I knew, I had one hero, my father. As a Christmas present to him when I was nine years old, I wrote the story of his life and titled it "My Hero." I had never had any trouble choosing my heroes, but it was an entirely different matter choosing my heroines. Except for Madame Curie, I had no female hero. Certainly not my mother, but I couldn't think of any reason why not. I loved her more than anything else in the world, but she wasn't my hero.

On the day that Colonel Marking and Yay came, I met the woman hero of my life. She was wearing a khaki shirt, khaki pants, and boots. She carried a holster and gun on her belt. Before the war, Yay had been a newspaper reporter and my mother's close friend. Yay talked in a very animated way, and I could listen to her for hours as she told of their adventures in the mountains. She and my mother often sat on the front porch, talking quietly together, but only when Colonel Marking was gone somewhere else. When he was home, he wanted Yay around him all the time, and he didn't want her talking to my mother by herself.

Yay and Colonel Marking stayed with us for some days. They also took our family with them on a PT boat to several islands to thank the people for their help during the guerrilla wars. It was on this trip, and the days they spent at our house, that I realized that Yay might not be very happy—she and Colonel Marking would fight often, in a more scary way than my parents fought because of the guns they carried. Several times they pointed their loaded guns at each other and threatened to shoot. But none of that stopped me from thinking of Yay as my hero. During the boat trip, she gave me a silver medal with her name on it.

After their visit with us, I thought about Yay often and about my mother. I felt badly that my mother was not my hero. One day, I went up to her as she was rocking on the front porch with Snuffy on her lap.

"Mommy. . . . ," I hesitated, but then continued, "Is it all right that Yay is my hero but you are not?"

She smiled at me and said, "Of course it's all right. Yay has a very adventurous life."

I felt a little better and asked if I could sit on her lap, too. I hadn't sat on her lap since I was small; in fact, I could not remember anytime that I had sat on her lap. Snuffy made room for me, and the three of us rocked silently.

"Can I always sit on your lap, even when I am 60 years old?" I asked my mother seriously.

She laughed and said, "When you are 60 years old you won't want to sit on my lap." She got up from the rocking chair, saying that we were getting too heavy, and went into the house. Snuffy and I looked at each other and knew instantly what we wanted to do. Snuffy got up and sat astride one arm of the rocker, while I did the same on the other arm, and we began rocking that chair as hard as we could, in time to a chant of "meow. . . . meow. . . . meow. . . ." In all this rocking and chanting, a question kept running around in my head. *Why hadn't my mother said "Yes," I could sit on her lap when I was 60 years old?*

All of a sudden, in the middle of our wild rocking and meowing, we heard a loud "CRACK"—one of the curved rockers had broken completely off! Snuffy and I got down off that rocker quickly and looked at the damage. There was no way we could fix it. My father did, later. He nailed two pieces of wood to hold the broken part in place, and after that, the rocker always rocked in a bumpy way. He wasn't angry at us. That's the way my father was— we could never tell what would make him angry. My mother was not that way—I always knew what would make her angry and what would make her cry and what would make her happy. But I didn't know what made her sad.

Snuffy and I would splash through the mud
puddles, singing our made-up songs.

19

School Days

During the years of the Japanese occupation when we lived in the foothills, Snuffy and I did not go to school. Instead, every morning before my parents left for work, my mother would give us schoolwork assignments. She made up addition and subtraction problems for Snuffy and assigned me pages from an arithmetic workbook. I loved arithmetic, and when I had finished the whole workbook, including long division and fractions, I would erase all the answers and start the book over again. During the morning, I would do the arithmetic and help Snuffy do hers. I also helped her read from some school readers and children's books. My brother was three years old (my sister was six and I was eight when we began doing this), but we played school with him and pretended he could read and write. By the end of the war, he **could** read and write, and my mother said it was all because we played school with him. I also had assignments in literature and history that came from a huge black book called "High School Self Taught." My father gave me, for my very own, a whole set of his books called "Historical Tales." My favorite volumes of that set were the two about King Arthur and the one about Russia.

We had five bookcases filled with my parents' books, and I was allowed to read any of them except the books in a bookcase that was kept locked. I did eventually sneak one book out when my father forgot to lock that bookcase. The book was called "The Sexual Life of Savages." I had wanted to read all about savages, and found very interesting things in that book. Most of the books in the other bookcases seemed very uninteresting to me. My father kept trying to get me to read a book called "The Republic" by Plato, and he said it would be interesting. I kept trying to read it but never got to any interesting part. The only thing I liked about the book was that the pages had a nice smell.

We didn't have much paper, and as the war went on we had less and less, until we had none at all. But my father gave me several hardback notebooks with black speckled covers, that he said was his "thesis" when he was at the University of California. All the pages of the notebooks were filled on one side with his scribble-scrabble writing in black ink, and he said I could use all the blank backsides of each page for my schoolwork. When my parents came home at night, my mother would look over our work and tell us what we did right and what we did wrong. For a special treat, she would bring home some brand new pencils, and it seemed to me that whenever I started my arithmetic with a brand new pencil, I wouldn't get anything wrong.

One day my mother brought home a book for me called "The Story of Mankind," by Henrik Wilhelm Van Loon. From the moment I started it, I did almost nothing else until I had finished it. Arithmetic was no longer my favorite subject—I had found real history. I read that book several times over. She also brought me books by Jean Henri Fabre about ants and other insects, which I read over and over.

Toward the end of the war, my mother stopped going into Manila—the long commute was too much for her in her weak condition. She opened a school in our house for the neighborhood children and called it the "San Juan Neighborhood School." Children came all day, some in the morning and some in the afternoon, because our house wasn't big enough for all the children to come at the same time. Their parents would bring vegetables, fruits, and old clothes to pay my mother for their children's schooling. Even if they couldn't pay, my mother would never turn away any child from her school. One child came from a rich family, and her parents paid my mother with money.

The only thing I didn't like about this was when I had to wear a pair of boy's short pants that had gotten too small for one of the older boys. Whenever I wore those pants (which I secretly liked because they had lots of pockets), the older kids would tease me by chanting, "Pooh is wearing Junior's pants! Pooh is wearing Junior's pants!" The teasing got worse when Junior gave me some green mangoes from a tree in his yard. Green mangoes are very sour, crunchy and very good when peeled and dipped in salt. Nothing can compare to eating a green mango with salt, sitting in the shade of a big tree, on a very hot afternoon. Except if you ate too many of them, you could get a pretty bad stomach ache by nightfall.

After the war ended, schools began to open again and my parents decided it was time that Snuffy and I went to a regular school. The government held examinations for all children to determine what grades the children should enter. During the four years of the war some children went to school and some didn't, so it was hard to know from the child's age into what grade that child should be placed.

I took the examination and qualified for the second year of high school. My parents said that I was too young to go to high school (I was 11), so they sent Snuffy and me to a school in San Juan called St. John's Academy, where the pupils were not divided into regular grades. We had to wear uniforms, a white shirt with a blue necktie and a dark blue skirt. The skirt didn't have any pockets. Worst of all, we had to wear shoes! I had worn no shoes for almost four years and they hurt my feet. I carried my shoes to school, put them on when we got there, and took them off before we started home. Snuffy didn't mind shoes—she liked her black shoes with the black bows.

The best thing about going to St. John's was walking to school with Snuffy. The school was about three miles away from our house, near the town of San Juan. When it was raining, we would splash through the mud puddles after Snuffy took off her shoes; she hated to have her pretty shoes muddy. On the way, we would pass a U.S. Army building with the long name "TECHNICAL IN-TELLIGENCE DEPOT" on a sign. We both thought that was a very impressive, great-sounding name, and we made up songs with different melodies but using the same words over and over, "Technical Intelligence Depot." When one of Snuffy's cats had kittens, we named one of them "Technical Intelligence Depot," pronouncing it with the "t" at the end of "Depot." My mother told us that the "t" was silent, so we called the cat "Depo" for short. Depo was a very sorry-looking kitten. She was born with something wrong with her two back legs. They wouldn't work, and the kitten would walk using only her front legs and dragging her two back legs behind. When it was time to give the kittens away, no one wanted Depo so we kept her. She became Snuffy's favorite cat.

It wasn't long before Snuffy found it very hard to keep walking the whole way to St. John's; she was sick very often, just as was my brother. Eventually, their illness was diagnosed as rheumatic fever and my sister had to go to a hospital to stay for a very long time, it seemed to me. I began to dislike going to St. John's, I didn't like wearing a uniform and I didn't like wearing shoes. The only thing I liked about St. John's was reading the poem, "Evangeline," by Henry Wadsworth Longfellow. I thought it was very sad and I loved it, except for the frustrating parts where Evangeline and Gabriel were looking for each other and kept missing each other.

The worst thing about going to St. John's was walking past the Technical Intelligence Depot without Snuffy. I told my mother that I didn't want to go to school anymore. She said I had to, but she would find another school for me in Manila. Eventually, she did. I went to two schools in Manila, at different times. The first one was the National Teacher's College, and the second was Bethel Girls High School.

At National Teacher's College (we called it NTC), I was put in an accelerated first-year high school class in which the entire first year of high school was covered in four months. I had a classmate named Terry who also lived in San Juan, and I rode to and from school with her in her uncle's jitney. They picked me up, and dropped me off, at a road intersection along the way. At NTC I finally learned algebra correctly. The algebra in the book from which I had tried to learn at home was confusing to me. I liked algebra because everything would work out perfectly in the end if you did it right.

In the school library, I discovered books by Jules Verne and Richard Halliburton. Jules Verne's books were fiction, mostly about voyages to strange places. My favorite of these stories was "Michael Strogoff"; it was about a very brave man in Russia. The Czar's men tried to blind him by putting hot coals near his eyes. I won't tell you how the story ended, in case you might want to read it someday.

Richard Halliburton's books were not fiction, they were about his travels all over the world where he often did crazy things. In Mexico, he jumped into a very deep pit where, in ancient times, young girls were made to jump as sacrifices to the Mayan Rain God. He did this just to find out what it would feel like to be a sacrifice to the Rain God.

Once, I tried to borrow a book called "Strange Fruit" by Lillian Smith—I had read that story in the army camp where the soldiers had paperback books, and I wanted to read it again—but the librarian wouldn't let me borrow it. She said it was not a good book for little girls to read, but she didn't say why. I thought to myself that there was only one advantage to being a grownup—you could read any book you wanted to read. There and then, I had a new ambition—to own a whole library myself when I grew up.

Something new that I had to get used to at NTC was boys. For as long as I could remember, wherever we lived, I fought the boys in my neighborhood—they were always my enemies. At NTC, we didn't have time to fight. The school day went from seven o'clock in the morning to noon (in the afternoon, there was another high school session for a different set of students). We had a 15-minute recess in the middle of the morning, when we could buy popsicles from the street vendor if any of us had any money. Sometimes, my father would give me five centavos to buy a popsicle at recess, and I could join the crowd around the popsicle vendor. My favorite kind of popsicle was corn—it was yellow and it had the flavor of corn and bits of boiled corn frozen into it.

I was very good in schoolwork. After every examination, the teacher would write on the board the names of the girl and boy students who had scored the highest on examinations. My name was written many times during those four months, along with the name of a boy, usually Guillermo Endriga. This made our classmates tease us, and they drew a heart around our names when the teacher stepped out of the room. I would get furious at this but there was nothing I could do but rush up to the board and erase the heart before the teacher came back in. One day, something curious happened. I looked at this boy when he wasn't looking at me, and discovered that every time I peeked at him, he was peeking back! I would turn away quickly and try not to peek at him again for a long time. He was a quiet boy, with black curly hair.

At the end of the four months, most of us were promoted to the second year of high school. To celebrate, there was a party in the school's quadrangle, a small open space in the middle of the school buildings. At the party, there was *calamansi* juice and cookies, and the principal made a little speech. Although we all knew each other from class, during the party all the girls gathered themselves in one corner near the refreshments table and all the boys gathered at another corner, pushing and shoving each other, and laughing. I don't know what possessed me, but I filled a glass with calamansi juice and carried it over to Guillermo Endriga. He looked rather startled, but took the glass from me and mumbled thank you. Very embarrassed, I went and hid among the other girls, who could not believe that I had actually done it. Neither did I. *Nor*

*could I have believed that, seven years later, Guillermo
Endriga and I would be married. From that marriage
came two beautiful daughters.*

During all the months that I stayed at that school,
Guillermo and I never spoke to each other. We did walk
almost side by side one very memorable day, July 4,
1946, when the United States granted the Philippines
its independence. Our class walked to the *Luneta*
where the Independence Day ceremonies were held.
We stood on the grass and watched the American flag
being lowered while the Star Spangled Banner was
played. Then the Philippine Flag was raised while the
band played our new national anthem, *Pambansang
Awit*. The melody was the same as our old one but the
words were new and in Tagalog instead of English. I
felt tingly all over as I watched the Philippine flag go
to the top of the flagpole. I was very proud that our
country was now really our own. Except for a few
months in 1898, when the Filipinos revolted against
Spain, for hundreds of years we had been ruled by
someone else—about 400 years by Spain, then 40 years
by the United States, then 4 years by Japan, and then
by the United States again. But not any more. *Many
years later, the Philippine Government changed the
day that Independence Day is celebrated—from July
4 when it was granted by the United States, to June 12
when the Filipinos declared it themselves in 1898.*

One day, my mother took me out of NTC and enrolled me in Bethel Girls High School. I made a new
friend named Rushelle, but I wished I could have stayed
at NTC. I didn't want to leave a school that I was just
getting used to, where I had friends, and where I was
falling in love with geometry. As it turned out, I didn't
stay at Bethel Girls High School long because my mother

became very sick and I had to stop going to school so
that I could take care of her.

I was furious, and attacked the biggest boy.

20

Bad Times

The bad times started for me when we were evicted from our house on Ortega Street. World War II had ended when Japan surrendered to the Allied Forces in August, 1945. The U.S. Army had dismantled their camps and had moved out of our neighborhood. We missed the friendly soldiers, the outdoor movies, the field kitchen leftovers and the C-rations. The Philippine government began rationing rice and canned sardines to the people because food was still scarce and few had money to buy any. Everyone was trying to find work and start over again. In Manila and in the other towns and cities, burned-out buildings were being cleared away and new ones built. U.S. Army jeeps were reappearing on the streets, decorated with painted flowers and designs of many colors. These "jeepneys" driven wildly by young men who paid no attention to traffic regulations, became public transportation. They still are.

I had to stand in long lines of people at the cockpit in the town of Mandaluyong for our ration of rice and canned sardines. I didn't mind because there were so many new things to see and hear in the town, which was about four miles down the hills from our house. The cockpit in the town was a huge open building with a corrugated iron roof and a hard compacted dirt floor. Under the roof, protected from the hot sun or pouring rain, vendors squatted selling boiled peanuts in their shells, boiled corn in their husks and corn roasting on hot coals, *bibingka* (rice cakes), and fresh *singkamas* (jicama). Small groups of old women also squatted near the vendors, chewing betel nut and spitting out red-colored saliva onto the ground. The women's teeth were black from many years of chewing betel nut. Sometimes the women would be smoking brown cigarettes, but not in the ordinary way. They would put the burning end of the cigarettes backwards into their mouths. I would watch them, fascinated that they didn't seem to get burned. Every so often, one would take the cigarette out of her mouth and flick a long tail of ash onto the ground.

In the middle part of the building were the cockfighting pits around which men squatted or stood, yelling, while they watched roosters fight. My father told me never to go near these cockfighting pits but, once, I couldn't stand not knowing what all the shouting was about so I squeezed in between the yelling men to look. I saw two roosters flying at each other, almost upright in the air, their neck feathers standing straight out. They were bleeding because small pointed knives were attached to their legs, and when they reached out to strike at each other with their claws, the knives would cut. I felt queasy and shaky, and crawled away. I never went near that part of the cockpit again.

One day, after I had returned home carrying our ration of rice and canned sardines, I found my parents upset. The owner of our house had come to say that he needed the house and we would have to move. I hadn't known until then that the house wasn't ours forever—I thought that because it had been looted, no one wanted it until my parents found it. But as it turned out, my parents had always known there was an owner; they had met the owner who was very glad to have someone stay in the house after it had been looted. At that time he had no money to fix the house. He was afraid that the house might be further vandalized if no one lived in it so he had let our family stay in it without paying rent. But now he had some money to fix it up so that he could rent it, and he told us to move out right away.

We had no place to go. My parents had no work and no salary, although my father kept looking in Manila for some kind of work, and he would make the long commute everyday. My mother was often sick, but my sister and brother were the sickest. They had rheumatic fever, and there came a time when they both had to stay for many weeks at a hospital in Manila, where my mother often stayed with them. When she herself was sick, my father or a friend would stay with them. I could seldom visit them because my parents needed me to take care of the house and stand in the long lines to collect our family ration of rice and canned sardines twice a week. They also insisted that I keep going to school. I missed Snuffy and Trotsky very much, and the house seemed so empty without them. I felt sorry that I had ever teased Snuffy about her cats—sometimes, when a cat would be yowling at night outside, I would tell my sister that it was one of her cats being eaten by a snake. She would believe me and cry.

Snuffy was my best friend. When we were little, we often squabbled, but as we grew, our squabbling became less and less. Before the war, when we still lived in Manila, Snuffy would take care of my doll, Margaret. I didn't like dolls very much nor did I play with them until I got Martha, but Snuffy did, and she would include Margaret when she took care of her own dolls. Snuffy and I often knew what each other was feeling without talking

*to each other. I took care of her because she was smaller
and not very strong, but she took care of me, too, in her
own way—when I needed someone to look up to me, or
to feel sorry for me, she was there. She would make me
little cards and notes and draw pictures for me, mostly
of people and flowers. Her drawings of people never had
any noses on them, but I liked them. Once, for my birthday, she made a fishing pole for me from a stick, some
string, and a bent nail for a hook. I didn't tell her that
the bent nail was too large a hook to catch anything, but
there weren't any fish in the streams or ponds, anyway.
During the dry season, the creeks and streams had
barely a trickle of water; during the rainy season, the
water flowed swiftly, but there were rarely any fish because they were all taken by the starving people. The
moment a fish would appear, even a tiny one, it was
taken quickly. I kept the fishing pole in my room, and
once in a while I took it with me when I went exploring
in the fields. I would tell Snuffy that I was going to catch
frogs with it.*

When Snuffy and Trotsky came back from the hospital I was very happy and promised to do everything they
wanted me to do. They had to continue to stay in bed so
I played quiet games with them, mostly checkers and
Chinese checkers and the Game of India (sometimes
called Parcheesi). I made paper dolls with cardboard
and cloth for Snuffy, and paper airplanes for Trotsky.
He would throw them into the air from his bed, and I
would chase them and bring them back to him. They loved
coloring books and "connect the dots" books, but these
were hard to find, so I would make dot pictures on paper for them to connect to see what picture would appear.

My father told the house owner that his children were
sick and we had no place to go, but the man didn't care.

He said if we were not out of the house by a certain date, some men would come and move our things out into the middle of the road. My father refused to move. He said the man had promised him four years ago that we could stay in the looted house as long as we wanted. But he didn't have anything in writing to prove it. My mother kept going out into the neighborhood and around the town of San Juan, looking for a place. But they all cost money, and we had none. She had friends who offered to let us stay with them, but that could be for only a few days because no one had much space.

The day finally came for the men to move our things out on the road. My father said they would never do it. My mother said they would, and we should be ready. She told me to collect all my things from my room downstairs and bring them to the living room. The men did come, and they began to move our furniture outside to the front yard. My father was yelling at them, but they kept doing it. My father said he would call the police but there were no police around to call. People in the neighborhood were all standing outside on the road, watching. I did not know what to do except hold my little brother's hand. Then my mother rushed in and said one of our neighbors would let us move into the space underneath their house. We could stay there as long as we wanted to, without paying any rent. I didn't feel good about this—I knew the place we would be going to. The people were Spanish, and their kids were not allowed outside their fence to play with the kids in the neighborhood. They would throw stones and spit at me whenever I passed their gate. But there was nothing I could do. All the neighbors helped carry our things to the new place. One of them told me that if I put a little grease on the cats in their new home, the cats would lick themselves clean and not try to go back to our old house. So

I rubbed the cats with grease as soon as I got them to the new place, they did wash themselves, and they did stay.

The new place had no walls and no doors. It was underneath the main house, and was open all around except at one side which had a concrete wall that was part of the supporting structure for the house. The open space was actually a driveway, but because of the house overhead, we had a ceiling. We were lucky the ceiling was just high enough to fit my father's bookcases underneath. One corner of the driveway against the concrete wall had been boarded up to make a small storeroom, and this became my parents' bedroom. Someone gave us old canvas tents, and we nailed them up to become the walls of our new place. These "walls" made it very hot because no breeze could get through, so we kept them rolled up and tied. In the typhoon season, the wind and rain would blow right in, and if it got too bad we would roll the canvas back down, even if it was stifling hot. My father didn't want his books nor our bedding and clothes to get soaking wet. I was more worried about my violin getting wet, so I would put it under my mattress during a storm.

In another corner of the driveway was a concrete septic tank with a "bathroom" built on top of it. This bathroom had no tiles, just a moldy concrete floor, rotting wooden walls, and a rusted toilet crusty all over with icky stuff; no matter how hard I scrubbed, the stuff wouldn't come off. When we put the large water drum in the bathroom, there was barely any space left in which to stand and take a bath. There was no kitchen but we set up our sawdust cooking stove along one side of the driveway, and put our round black table in the middle. We had two electric lights from the U.S. Army's generator for the neighborhood, but no running water or gas. My mother put the lace tablecloth on the table, and I got some flowers in a can as a centerpiece, and the place began to look nice and cozy. We lined the beds up against the concrete wall; the cats jumped on them right away and curled up.

Times got worse. Although my parents found work in Manila so we had some money again, it became a source of trouble between them. My mother would turn over all her little salary to my father, but he was very suspicious and thought that she was keeping some of it. I knew she wasn't, and I felt very angry at my father—his suspicions would make my mother cry. It hurt me very much to see her cry. My mother never had any money except what my father gave her for her transportation and food for the family. One day, I did something I had never done before—I took one peso (about the same as one dollar) from my father's wallet when he was not in his room, and I put the peso deep in my mother's big purse. I was afraid that my father would notice the peso missing because he kept his money in different compartments of his wallet and knew exactly how much he had in each compartment. But there was no blowup for days after I took that peso, so sometime later I did it again. And again. I was frightened each time, but because I didn't do it very often, and always took only one peso, neither of my parents ever knew that I did this. There were so many things in my mother's purse, and she frequently rummaged around in it looking for some money, so I guess she was never surprised to find a peso bill among all her stuff. I did not know what she did with those extra pesos—I imagined that she would buy ice cream or cookies or lipstick when she was away at work.

I knew that taking those pesos from my father's wallet was wrong, but at that time, from my 12-year-old point of view, there was something even more wrong—my mother's tears. I grew to dislike money because of all the trouble it caused between my parents.

Then Trotsky had to go back into the hospital to stay for a long time, and my mother got sicker. I stopped going to school so that I could take care of her. My father's job was in Manila, so he could see my brother everyday. One day, my mother got so sick that she had to be taken to the hospital in Manila. My father would get home very late after that because he was visiting both my brother and my mother, who were in different hospitals. Snuffy and I would sit near the gate and wait for him after I covered his supper with another plate. Because of his night blindness, he needed to be guided after he got down from the caretella which would drop him off at the street corner or sometimes at our gate. He would tell us that our mother and brother were doing well.

These were the times when I had my worst fistfights in the neighborhood. The neighborhood boys would tease me and I would get so angry I would chase them and get into fights. My father had taught me to fight when I was little; he had been a varsity boxer in college. He didn't like me to fight—he always said I should "reason" with my enemies. But he also said not to run away; if I had to fight, then I should fight "properly" so he taught me. But the neighborhood boys didn't fight properly, nor did I feel like "reasoning" with them. When someone teases you, you can't reason with them, you can only fight them. My mother would say, if someone teases you, just walk away. But I could never walk away because I would get so angry. My mother said that I must have inherited my father's Visayan temper.

I would also get very angry when the Spanish kids who lived in the house above us would lean out their upstairs windows, wait for me to come out from under the house, and then spit on me. I hated this and wanted to shoot stones at their windows with my slingshot, but my parents said that I must be nice to them because they were letting us live under their house without paying rent. *I was learning something else about money— if you had enough to pay your own rent, other people wouldn't treat you like dirt.*

One evening, before my father had gotten home, my sister and I were waiting for him as usual, when a group of boys came up to us in the road and said nasty things to me. I was furious and attacked the biggest boy, who was a head taller than I was. My sister began to cry, but I was too angry to pay attention to her. The boy began to laugh and started hitting me on the chest. That hurt, which shocked me. The other boys urged him on, telling him to keep hitting me on the chest. My eyes were stinging with tears and I could hardly see, but I kept hitting him as hard as I could, while trying to protect my chest.

Some men came up to us and squatted in the road, laughing. They also told the big boy where to hit me. I was hurt very badly. I fell in the road several times, but kept getting up to keep fighting. My sister was crying, asking me to please stop and go home. Then one of the men stood up and said *"Tama na!"* ("That's enough") to the big boy. They all got up and went away, laughing. I stood there, panting and crying from anger and frustration because of how they were laughing at me. I hurt all over as Snuffy and I stumbled back to our house. She had dried her tears and was saying that Daddy would be mad if he knew I was fighting. I told her not to tell him, and that he couldn't see that I had been fighting, anyway. I washed myself up as best as I could.

My father came home and said that my mother needed me to take care of her in the hospital. She had just had a major operation that day and there were not enough nurses. The next day he took me to the hospital.

21

The Philippine
General Hospital

The hospital where my mother had to stay for her
operation, and for more than a month afterwards, was
in Manila and was called "PGH" for short. Two big
white crosses were painted on the roofs of the buildings as a sign to bombers that this was a hospital—in
wartime, hospitals were not supposed to be bombed.
During the liberation of Manila by the Americans, the
Japanese put healthy soldiers into the hospital because
they knew the Americans would not bomb a building
with a white cross on the roof. However, the Americans found out about the Japanese soldiers and bombed
the hospital anyway. So after the war had ended, at
the time my mother had to be in the hospital, it had
not yet been rebuilt. Just the concrete walls and floors
were still standing, pocked with holes from shrapnel
and bomb fragments. New roofs had been put on, and
large canvas sheets had been hung up to keep out the
rain and wind during typhoons. Just as in our home,
this made the inside very hot and stifling, so most of
the time the canvas was rolled up and tied with huge
ropes.

My mother's bed was in the women's ward, a huge room with 25 to 30 beds on each side of the long room, each bed perpendicular to the walls and facing the center aisle. Between each bed was a white metal stand with one drawer, and a shelf with a wash basin. On each stand was a white enamel pitcher with drinking water. There was just enough space between each bed for a person to walk or stand. At night, I would spread a narrow mat on the floor between my mother's bed and the next one, and sleep there. I would wake up when my mother called to me for a cup of water or for a bedpan. (When a patient is too sick or weak to get out of bed to go to the bathroom, she has to use a small metal pan brought to her bed). A number of bedpans were kept in a room at the end of the ward. There was a toilet in that room, and a deep sink with running water from a faucet to be used to rinse out the bedpan after I had poured the contents into the toilet and flushed it. Sometimes, there was no water coming from the faucet, or for flushing the toilet. There were big drums, like the one we had at home, with water and a *tabo* (large dipper) for rinsing out the bedpan and flushing the toilets. That room had a very bad smell, but it was cleaned only once a day.

Almost every patient in the ward had someone in their family taking care of them because there were so few nurses in the whole hospital. At meal times an orderly would wheel in huge carts with trays of food for each patient, and the family members would take the tray with their patient's name on it. After I fed my mother, I would go to the end of the ward where there was a big pot of rice and another pot of vegetables, and sometimes fish, for the family members. I would put food on my mother's plate, carry it back to her bed and eat beside her. The food was good. My father would come every day to visit, bringing bananas or *narangheta* (native oranges) for my mother, who shared them with the patients in the beds next to hers.

I knew that my father was missing my mother very much. Despite their many fights, they loved each other. At home, they would spend a long time at the table after meals, discussing their work, their opinions, and events in the country and the world. They agreed on many things, such as the rich being too rich and often taking advantage of poor people—it seemed to them that the rich were getting richer and the poor were getting poorer. My parents didn't always agree on how to change that—my father would say that the poor people should revolt as they did against the Czar in Russia. My mother did not believe in violence; she thought that the rich should share with the poor. Against my father's wishes she would sometimes invite in beggars who came to our door and would share with them what little food and clothing we had. My father did not like this at all. He said people were taking advantage of my mother, that we had very little ourselves, and that poor people had too many children and expected God to take care of everything. During those at-the-table discussions, we children would get bored listening, but my parents never seemed to tire of talking to each other.

The best time of day in the hospital was early in the morning. The sunshine would come in through the big openings in the walls, but it was not very hot yet. The birds would sing in the trees outside, and the cool morning breeze would bring in fresh smells to drive out the bad hospital smells that seemed to get worse at night. Everyone knew breakfast was coming and would get ready for it. All the patients seemed to like mealtimes best; there was always a feeling of anticipation just before the meal cart would come in, even though everyone knew what the food would be. The family members would line up for bedpans and get wet cloths to wipe the patients' faces. We would all talk and greet each other and stretch, glad to get up off that hard concrete floor. I would take down the mosquito net over my mother's bed and bring a cool, wet cloth to wipe her face. I would kiss her forehead, and she would smile and give me a kiss on my cheek. She was getting stronger every day.

The best part I looked forward to was the doctors' rounds. They would come in groups, going from one bed to the next. There was usually a main doctor, and a couple of others, with the head nurse. I liked the rounds best because I wanted to be sure that my mother was getting better, and only the doctor could tell us. The doctor would examine my mother, talk to her, and explain things to the other doctors and to the head nurse. Then he would tell my mother that she was doing very well. I would feel light as a feather when I heard him say that. She always asked when she could go home, and he would say "soon." Later, the head nurse would come back and see my mother several times during the day; her name was Miss Malong, and she knew my mother from before the war. She would also talk to me and tell me what a good job I was doing taking care of my mother. Sometimes, she brought a sweet biscuit for me.

My mother slept most of the day. I would fan her to help her sleep better and to keep the flies from bothering her. Sometimes, I visited some of the other patients to talk with them or bring their bedpans if their family members were away for awhile.

Nighttime was the worst time in the hospital. Most of the lights would be turned off except at the end of the ward where the nurses desk was, and it would be very hot. The family members would hang the mosquito nets on their patients' beds, and it would get hotter for them under the nets. I would try to fan my mother through the net, but I would get sleepy and doze off sometimes, even with the mosquitoes biting me.

The worst thing about the nights were the moans and cries of the patients. Maybe the dark scared them, or they were afraid because the doctors had gone home. Sometimes, if one patient was moaning and shouting out very loudly, the other patients would yell at her to keep quiet. The night nurse would come in and try to calm the patients who were moaning the loudest. Lying on the floor on my mat, I would wake up several times during the night, not only when my mother called me but if someone screamed. In my head, I imagined how good it would feel when morning came again.

Finally, the day came when my mother could go home. My father came to get us, bringing one of my mother's dresses, and I packed up her things in a small bag. I said good-bye to the patients and their families that I had known the best. Miss Malong took us to the hospital door. It was so good to step out into the fresh air and sunshine again, and to go home.

When we got home, I found that my brother was home from his hospital, too. We were all together again, and I was happy.

22

My Vacations

Sometime after we had come home from the hospital my mother said that Miss Malong had invited me to spend a vacation with her in the Nurses Home on the hospital grounds. She said Miss Malong thought that I needed a vacation and some rest and good food. I liked Miss Malong but I didn't want to leave my family, not even for a week, nor did I feel like resting. My parents both said I should go. My mother bought me a new white shirt to wear during my vacation. So I went, even though I didn't want to.

Miss Malong's room in the Nurses Home was neat and quiet; there were two beds in it, and at night the sheets felt so cool and clean. I even had a pillow and a pillowcase. Her room was on the second or third floor, right next to big acacia trees. There were bars on the windows, but I could sit on the polished wooden windowsill and watch the trees rustling in the breeze and the main avenue outside the hospital grounds.

At first, I liked my vacation. I liked the cool and quiet, sitting in the window watching the trees, not doing anything. But after one day, I was homesick. I had to stay in Miss Malong's room all day while she was doing her nursing duties. She would come and get me at

noon and take me to eat in the nurses' dining room; we
also had breakfast and supper there. I liked that best. I
liked sitting at the tables covered with white tablecloths
with all the nurses, and talking to them and listening to
them. There were real glasses on the table, and water
with ice in it. The food was delicious, and there was always dessert. Sometimes, several of the nurses would
give me their dessert, but Miss Malong said I shouldn't
have too much. The nurses obeyed her. They whispered
to me that Miss Malong was the strictest head nurse in
the whole hospital and that even the doctors were afraid
of her. Miss Malong was strict with me, too. She said I
must brush my teeth after each meal, even after I went
home. She said it very nicely to me. She had a different
tone in her voice when she talked to me than when she
talked to the nurses. I didn't have a toothbrush—at
home, I used a fresh twig with salt each morning for
brushing my teeth. Miss Malong gave me a new toothbrush and she said I could take it home.

But as nice as Miss Malong was, and as good as the
food was, I wanted to go home. I didn't want to hurt her
feelings, so I didn't say anything about that to her and
stayed there a whole week. It seemed very much longer
than that.

Some months later, my parents sent me on another
vacation. This time it was to the province where, they
said, I would be able to ride horses. One of their friends,
a young woman named Mickey, was going for a few days
to her hometown and suggested I come with her and
have a vacation. Again, I didn't want to go, and again, I
had to go. It turned out to be the wrong time for a vacation of riding horses. It happened to be the end of "Holy
Week" for Catholics (the week just before Easter), and
the family whose house I stayed in said that it would be
a sin (something bad) to ride horses or to do anything

else, on Holy Thursday or Holy Friday. So I sat in their house, looking out the window at the two small horses nibbling grass outside. On Saturday, people were allowed to do things again, so before we boarded the bus to go home, Mickey let me ride one of the horses around the outside of the house for a few minutes.

On the way home on the bus, Mickey asked me if I had a good vacation. I said yes because I didn't want to hurt her feelings. But I wished to myself that I wouldn't ever have to go on a vacation again—except, of course, if I could go in a big ship, with huge sails, on the ocean. I was 12 years old, and still in love with the sea.

"I must go down to the seas again, to the lonely
sea and the sky, and all I ask is a tall ship and a
star to steer her by . . ."

23

The Sea, At Last

"I must go down to the seas again, to the lonely sea and the sky,
And all I ask is a tall ship, and a star to steer her by,
And the wheel's kick and the wind's song, and the white sail's shaking,
And a grey mist on the sea's face and a grey dawn breaking."

"I must go down to the seas again, for the call of the running tide
Is a wild call and a clear call that cannot be denied;
And all I ask is a windy day with the white clouds flying,
And the flung spray and the blown spume, and the sea-gulls crying."

"I must go down to the seas again to the vagrant gypsy life,
To the gull's way and the whale's way where the wind's like a whetted knife;
And all I ask is a merry yarn from a laughing fellow-rover,
And quiet sleep and a sweet dream when the long trick's over."

"Sea-Fever," by John Masefield

"Sea Fever" was my favorite poem. I had copied it from my mother's book of poetry onto a piece of brown paper and pasted a picture of the ocean on the paper. With a thumbtack, it had hung on the wall of my sloping room on Ortega Street as long as we lived there and when we moved, I folded it away in one of my cigar boxes because there was no place to hang it in the driveway we moved into. Every once in a while, I took it out of the box, unfolded it, and read the poem, although I had already memorized it. The poem had to go with the picture to feel right.

I was almost 13 years old when my mother's father, who was living in Canada, sent money for us to come to the United States so that my mother and brother could get medical treatment. By "us" my grandfather did not mean my father, but my parents' friends contributed enough money to buy him an airplane ticket to the United States. I had never seen my grandfather, nor did he ever write to us until then. Many years before, he had not wanted my mother to marry my father, and when she did, he never communicated with her again. But the snapshot taken by that soldier (his stepson), and my mother's letter to him at the same time, seemed to have changed his mind. However, he did not want to see us, he only wanted us to get medical treatment.

We could bring only our clothes to America because we didn't know where we would be staying. We packed the rest of our personal belongings into the huge black trunk that we had always used as a small table. My mother said this was the trunk that she and my father had with them when they eloped to the Philippines in 1930, after she graduated from the University of California at Berkeley. She and my father had met there while they were both students.

I was sorry to have to pack my little doll, Martha, in the trunk along with my books. When I was about seven years old, one of my mother's friends had given me this little doll, who was about five inches tall, with brown hair, wearing a red dress, a white, frilly petticoat, and a red bonnet. I loved her the moment I saw her, and named her after a little orphan girl in the Heidi books.

Before Martha came into my life, I had never liked dolls, and especially did not like big dolls. In fact, I was almost afraid of them. When I would go downtown with my mother and had to pass a store window with manni-kins in them, I would shut my eyes tightly until I was sure we were past the window. I did not like seeing man-nikins nor dolls. But Martha was different. She was small and would look at me in her gentle way. She and I had often played quietly by ourselves on the landing half-way up the stairs in our house in Manila. As I grew older, I stopped playing with her but she stayed in her wicker basket on the beam in my sloping room; once in a while I would take her out of her basket, smooth her dress and talk to her.

I kissed Martha goodbye before I wrapped her care-fully in a piece of cloth and put her in her basket. I told her I would be back in one year. I had to throw away my slingshot and all my cigar boxes of pretty stones and other collections because the family who was going to keep my father's bookcases of books and the black trunk had no space for all our things. My mother gave my vio-lin away, but promised to get me a new one, full-sized, when we got to America. We gave away all our bedding and dishes and pots and pans but kept our silverware, the lace tablecloth and family photographs from before the war in the black trunk. We gave away all our furni-ture, some of which was so broken that it was going to be used for firewood.

My parents were very excited and happy about our coming trip. They told us we would be able to buy new things in America, even bicycles. A bicycle! In my mind's eye I pictured a shiny, new red bicycle. *I had never had a bicycle but my father had taught me to ride one when I*

*was about six years old; the bicycle belonged to one of
the boys who had boarded with us before the war.* But
the best part of going to America was that my little
brother, whose rheumatic fever might have damaged
his heart, would be cured, and whatever sickness my
mother had would be fixed. And my father's eyes might
also be fixed to see better again because doctors in
America were discovering new cures and medicines
everyday. By then, my father was almost totally blind.

And I would be on the sea, at last. The cheapest
way to cross the Pacific Ocean to America was on a
freighter. The trip would take one month because the
ship had to stop at several ports to load and unload cargo.
The freighter belonged to the American President Lines
and was named the "President Pierce"; it was bound
for San Francisco, California, via Hong Kong, China,
and Honolulu, Hawaii. When I saw the ship, it did not
matter that there were no sails. It was painted gray
and very big, with different colored flags flying from the
masts. On the ship, mysterious smells and sounds surrounded me. To this day, the smell of a ship brings back
all the excitement and bustle and anticipation of the day
the President Pierce sailed with my mother, my sister,
my brother, and me. My mother taught us this fragment
of a song:

"San Francisco, open your golden gate,
Don't let the stranger wait,
Outside your door!"

We sang it when the ship entered San Francisco Bay.
I never saw my mother look so young, and beautiful,
and excited, and happy as on that day.

When I would return to Manila, I would be 14 years
old. Ahead of me in America I would discover the won-

ders of trigonometry and chemistry, the pleasures of playing second violin in the orchestra at Balboa High School in San Francisco, and the magic of Mendelssohn, Tchaikovsky, Mozart, and Beethoven on phonograph records. I did not know any of that was going to happen when I boarded the gangway of the President Pierce. I was about to go to sea, not in the way I had daydreamed about, but it was enough.

The End

Passport photograph, 1946. Snuffy age 10,
Trotsky age 7, Pooh age 12.

ADDENDA

What Happened to Everybody?

Felipe and Doreen

Something About the Philippines

What Happened to Everybody?

In America, the Gamboa family was split up among friends in the San Francisco Bay area; as visitors in the United States, Felipe and Doreen were not allowed to work and thus had no means of supporting their family. This fragmentation of her family was very difficult for Pooh. Eventually, Doreen found part-time work in an elementary school in San Francisco and the family was able to live together again, first in a tiny apartment on Geary Street, then in an attic apartment on Scott Street. The family returned to the Philippines in August of 1948 after spending a year and a half in America.

While in California, Trotsky spent a year in a convalescent hospital in Belmont, where his rheumatic fever was treated. He grew up healthy, but was not allowed to participate in high school sports. He had a rough time as a teen-ager, fighting frequently with his parents, drinking too much alcohol, and failing almost all his classes in high school despite a very high IQ. To change his life, his parents sent him to Weber State College in Utah where he did very well and stopped drinking. He graduated with a degree in Business Administration and is now an Area Sales Manager in Florida for a global building materials company. He is married and has two grown daughters, Lisa and Tina. His best times are spent fishing the backwaters of Pine Island, Florida, and watching the sunsets with his wife, Rhonda, from their stilt home overlooking the water. Every once in a while he sends Pooh *calamansi* and *guava* fruits that grow in his yard.

Snuffy was popular in high school and graduated as Salutatorian. Like Trotsky, her childhood illness with rheumatic fever prevented her from participating in competitive sports but she excelled in water ballet. She went on to the University of the Philippines for her college degree in Business Administration and a master's degree in Industrial Management. She was very active in the university's drama group. Soon after graduation, she married one of her professors, Cesar Virata. They have three children, Steven, Gillian, and Michael, and four grandchildren: Enzo, Daniella, Javier, and Diego. All except Michael live in the Philippines. With Pooh and Trotsky living in the United States, Snuffy alone took care of their mother, who became ill with cancer. She also took care of their father whose blindness made him quite dependent on her. After her mother died, Snuffy joined a repertory group and began a life on the stage where her talents blossomed after long being held back. She continues to act in plays, sings and dances in musicals and also organizes and directs children's theater in Manila. She still has cats. About every two years, she comes to the United States and visits Pooh, who still misses her sister.

Pooh had a difficult teen-age life, no longer a "perfect" child, sometimes running away from home, but always finding comfort in classical music recordings and in nature. She built model airplanes and read avidly, particularly the authors Feodor Dostoevsky, Leo Tolstoy, and William Faulkner. She was a varsity swimmer and the Manila champion in the 100-meter backstroke. She took 2nd place in the Philippine national championships

in the same event, losing 1st place to a German girl by a
tenth of a second. (Pooh never forgave herself for this
loss until she became a grandmother). Pooh's parents
did not approve of competitive sports in general, and
Pooh's swimming in particular, but they could not stop
her from competing. Despite his disapproval and his
blindness, Pooh's father attended almost every swimming meet; her mother attended none, including the national championships. Snuffy, on the other hand, supported her sister whole-heartedly and was at all the
meets.

Pooh graduated from the Philippine Women's University with a degree in Chemistry, *magna cum laude*,
at the age of nineteen. She married Guillermo Endriga
that same year, against the wishes of her parents. From
that marriage, she has two daughters, Gilita Star and
Marya Curie, now grown and with children of their own:
Gilita and her husband Patrick Thomas have twins,
Cecilia and Christopher; Marya and her husband Todd
Hirsch have a daughter, Marika, and a son, Michael.
Pooh's marriage to Guillermo broke up when their daughters were little. After graduation from college, Pooh's
first job was as a chemist in the Bureau of Soils in Manila. She held this job for eight years, during which time
she became involved in soils experimental research and
set up the Bureau's first Radioisotope Laboratory. In
1961, she entered graduate school with a scholarship in
Soil Science at the University of California in Berkeley,
earning her doctoral degree in 1971. While in graduate
school, she met and married Roy Lewis, a physics stu-
dent who is now a scientist at the University of Chi-
cago. Pooh had intended to return to the Philippines after graduate school but her marriage to Roy changed
that—divorce and re-marriage are not legal in the Philippines. Pooh and Roy have been married more than 34

years; they have a son, Stephen, who lives in San Francisco with his wife, Barbara Pollak, the illustrator of this book. Pooh is a professor of environmental engineering at Northwestern University in Evanston, Illinois. Some years ago she became a Jew. She finds great delight in the similarities between searching for truth in science and in Talmudic arguments. In between her scientific work, her teaching, and the study of Talmud and Hebrew, she still enjoys reading history books and still takes violin lessons.

Felipe and Doreen

Pooh's father, Felipe, was born on September 30, 1899 or 1900, in Iloilo on the island of Panay in the Visayan Islands. Felipe never knew his parents because they died when he was still a baby. His father was killed in the Philippine-American war, when the Filipinos were fighting to prevent the United States from taking over their country. His mother died of an illness soon after. In those days, people tended to die young from diseases for which there were no cures. Felipe had an older sister who caught typhoid fever when she was a young girl; she recovered but suffered some brain damage. Felipe also had five half-sisters from his father's first marriage; these sisters were much older than he and were more like his aunts than his sisters. After the death of his parents, his half-sisters, who had children of their own, could not take care of him and Felipe was raised in a Catholic convent by nuns. His life was miserable there, according to him. When he was 12 years old, Felipe persuaded one of his half-sisters, Inday Fe, to let him live with her. He was happy in her house; he liked playing with Inday Fe's children, he had spending money and good clothes, and Inday Fe sent him to school. He had not been to school before, so he entered first grade at the age of 12. He was so bright, however, that before the year ended, he was put into Grade 5. He was a fast runner as well as a fast learner, and when he entered

Iloilo High School he joined the track team. He was also elected president of the freshman class.

At the end of his freshman year in high school, Felipe met a man who persuaded him to go to America where he could find a much better life. He approached his aunts and half-sisters for the money for the boat trip and he promised never to bother them again. Inday Fe was sad that he wanted to leave to go to America—she had hoped that he would learn to manage her *hacienda* (a large farm growing sugar cane). But Felipe had not liked the way the farm laborers were treated, and he knew he would not enjoy becoming the farm manager some day. His aunts and half-sisters gave him the money, and the man, named Abelarde, took him to Manila where the ship would sail for America. The day they were to leave, however, Abelarde became ill and could not go. Felipe, who was only 15 years old at the time, sat on the pier and cried, not knowing what to do. When he finished crying, he decided to go to America by himself.

The ship he was on landed in San Francisco. He found work as a houseboy and as a busboy in restaurants, he picked fruit on farms, and he went to school. He finished high school, excelling in English and mathematics. After his high school graduation, he went to work in the forests of Oregon as a cook for a team of lumberjacks; he also worked in arsenic mines and in canning factories. He wanted to continue his schooling in college, so he got a job as a hospital orderly in Eugene, Oregon, and enrolled at the University of Oregon from which he graduated with a Bachelor's degree. While in college he learned to box and was on the University of Oregon's varsity boxing team and tennis team. Throughout his life and in all the houses in which he lived, Felipe's banner from the University of Oregon hung on the wall of his study. It became moth-eaten, dusty, and bedraggled, but he never threw it away.

While working as a hospital orderly during college, Felipe met an older woman who was a patient in the hospital. She took a liking to him and admired his determination to earn a college degree. She decided to adopt him officially, and from then on he carried her last name, Brewster, as his mother's name. He loved his adopted mother almost as a son; she was the only mother he had known. When she died, Mrs. Brewster left him her house in Oregon. He eventually sold the house so that he could go to graduate school at the University of California in Berkeley. He chose to concentrate on studies in political science and sociology. He kept a small framed picture of himself with Mrs. Brewster and another young man on one of his bookcases. Over many years the picture faded, but even when Felipe lost his eyesight, he continued to keep the picture on his bookcase.

At the University of California in Berkeley, Felipe met Doreen, Pooh's mother. Doreen was born in Stanger, South Africa, on September 8, 1907. Her father, George Sidney Barber, was a Presbyterian minister of English-Scottish descent. He was in Africa to convert Africans to become Presbyterians and to administer to a Presbyterian parish. Doreen's mother, Grace Stewart Barber, was Irish and had been born in Moneydarragh, Ireland. Doreen had a younger brother, James, also born in South Africa.

When Doreen was about five years old, her mother died. George Sidney moved his family to Canada, then to Texas, then to Globe, Arizona. In Globe, when Doreen was about 12 years old, her father met and married a woman with two children, Dick and Rosemary. Doreen thought that her stepmother was the most beautiful woman she had ever seen and grew to love her very much. When Doreen was 16 years old, the family moved to Tracy, California. Although there was about a 10-year difference in age between Doreen and her younger stepsister Rosemary, they became close friends and loved each other very much. For all the years that Pooh was growing up, Doreen often talked about Rosemary; she seldom talked about her brother Jim (who had been strongly against her marriage to Felipe), except to say that he had been a car racing driver in England and had invented carmel corn. She once said that her step-brother, Dick, grew up to be very much like her father and also became a Presbyterian minister.

Doreen graduated from Tracy High School and went on to the University of California in Berkeley. She enrolled in a premedical program because she wanted to become a doctor. She was active in one of the University groups that was centered in the Protestant religion, and often gave talks at the meetings. It was at one of these meetings that she met Felipe—he was there out of curiosity, to see what kind of people went to those meetings. He belonged to no church and held the opinion that religion led to the oppression of people. At one of the meetings, he heard one young woman (Doreen) give a spirited talk that piqued his interest—he went up to her afterwards and introduced himself.

Thus began the life that Felipe and Doreen would share together. They each had strong opinions that did not often agree—as Doreen told Pooh, "we quarreled daily and made up on weekends!" Eventually, they decided to get married. Doreen's father was absolutely opposed to the marriage—he did not want his daughter marrying a Filipino, a dark-skinned foreigner. The young couple had no alternative—in 1930 they eloped by ship to the Philippines, where Felipe believed he would have the money to support a family because he had an inheritance from his parents that was being held for him until he returned. Felipe was still writing his dissertation and Doreen had just graduated with her Bachelor of Arts degree and was about to begin medical school. Because of their elopement to the Philippines, Felipe never completed his doctorate in political science, and Doreen never became a medical doctor.

When the young couple disembarked from the ship in Manila, Felipe immediately tried to contact his older sister, Luisita, who had been in charge of his share of the inheritance from their parents. He was told that there was no money left, that his sister had spent it all and was living in poverty with a child. Felipe could do nothing about this, but he became very angry at his sister and refused to have anything more to do with her for the rest of his life. Over the years of Pooh's growing up, Luisita would occasionally come to the Gamboa house. It was obvious even to Pooh as a child that there was something the matter with her aunt's mind, most likely the result of Luisita's illness with typhoid fever . Pooh's family moved several times over the years, from one rented house to another, but Luisita always managed to find them; Doreen (Luisita called her "Doie") always welcomed her. When Pooh was around two years old, Luisita brought her son to Doreen and begged her to take care of him for a while. Doreen could never turn children away, and agreed—somehow, she was able to convince Felipe that it was the thing to do. Pooh does not remember the time that her cousin Felix lived with the family, but there were pictures of him in the family album.

Finding themselves with very little money to start off their lives in the Philippines, Felipe and Doreen looked for work right away. Felipe began writing articles for a newspaper, worked as a researcher at the

Institute of Pacific Relations, and then became a college professor in political science and sociology at the Philippine Women's University. Doreen worked at several part-time, temporary jobs during those first years: salesgirl for children's books in the Philippine Education Company during the Christmas rush, dormitory counselor in the YWCA, history teacher at a Chinese school, and teacher at the National Teachers College. Because she was a "white" woman who had become a Filipino citizen, she was told that she was "out of place" in terms of a permanent job. Then, in 1937, she was hired as a full-time nursery school and kindergarten teacher at the Philippine Women's University where Felipe was a professor.

The young couple decided not to have children right away because they thought they needed to have more money and a better place to live. They were still saying this when Pooh was born on January 9, 1934. Snuffy was born two years later, on January 18, 1936, and Trotsky on March 13, 1939. A baby boy was born in 1940, but he lived only 24 hours; his parents named him Jose Rizal after the Philippine national hero.

Soon after Pooh was born, Felipe's half-sister, Inday Fe, offered to adopt the baby and raise her on the hacienda in Iloilo. This was not an unusual offer in the Philippines – Inday Fe believed that Felipe and Doreen did not have enough money or space to raise a child, and she wanted to help the young couple in the only way she knew how. Pooh's parents refused the offer as gently as they could; they knew that Inday Fe meant well and didn't want to hurt her feelings.

After World War II, while the Gamboa family was in California for a year and a half, Doreen enrolled at Mills College and earned her Master's Degree in Child Development. Upon returning to the Philippines in 1948, she took over the position of head of the elementary school at the Philippine Women's University. She became very well known in the Philippines for her methods of teaching children; teachers came from all over the country to learn from her. She established another school for the Philippine Women's University in Quezon City. The school was called the Jose Abad Santos Memorial School, and it included a complete high school besides a nursery school, kindergarten, and elementary school. Doreen wrote two books on the Filipino child – one was published in 1972, entitled "The Filipino Child as Viewed by Self and Others." The other book, "Learning To Be Free," was published through Snuffy's efforts after Doreen died of cancer in 1977.

Doreen's contributions to education in the Philippines were officially recognized in 1976, when she received the Presidential Award for Education from the Philippine government, and the Doctor of Pedagogy degree, *honoris causa*, from the Philippine Women's University.

Felipe's life after World War II was taken over by his increasing, and ultimately total, blindness. He continued to be on the faculty at the Philippine Women's University, teaching sociology and political science, and acting as advisor for graduate students working on their theses. He refused to learn Braille because, he said, anything he wanted to read was not available in Braille. Instead, he hired young students to read to him. He put several such students through college that way. He taught himself to type because he continued to work on writing his book. However, he became frustrated at the slowness of his typing and eventually turned to dictating his words to the hired students. Although he was very careful of his health and lived to be 92 years old, he died before he finished his book. After his death, Snuffy tried to have the manuscript edited and completed, but the material he left behind was filled with statistics, too difficult and disorganized for someone else to finish. Over his lifetime, however, he did publish several articles. One day, after Pooh had grown up and was working as a chemist in the Bureau of Soils in Manila, Felipe told her that he had gone to the reference library at the Bureau of Science to look up his name in the card catalog of publications. His name was gone, he said, but her name was in its place. He seemed rather proud that this had happened.

Felipe and Doreen were very different people, but they had at least one characteristic in common: they stuck to their principles.

Something About
The Philippines

On a map, you can find the Philippines just above the equator—it looks a little like a sea horse. The Pacific Ocean is on the east side of the Philippines, and the South China Sea is on the west side. The nearest countries are Taiwan, China, Vietnam, and Malaysia. The Philippines is actually an archipelago (a group of many islands) consisting of more than 7,000 islands. The biggest islands are Luzon in the north and Mindanao in the south; a long, thin island, Palawan, sticks out into the China Sea. The capital city, Manila, is on Luzon. The Philippines is located in the Tropics (the region around the Earth's equator) and has two seasons, "wet" and "dry." The temperatures remain about the same during both seasons—very hot! During the wet season (around June to November), it rains heavily and almost continuously, often resulting in flooded homes and streets. This is also the season for typhoons, very strong rain and winds that can knock down trees and light poles, and carry off the roofs of houses. Typhoons are very similar to hurricanes—both are tropical cyclones—but typhoons start in the West Pacific region of the world whereas hurricanes start in the West Indies region. During the dry season in the Philippines (around December to June), there is almost no rain.

Archeological evidence indicates that about 450,000 years ago, a species of people, *homo erectus*—similar to our human species (*homo sapiens sapiens*)—crossed land bridges from the mainland of Asia into the Cagayan Valley on the island of Luzon. Other evidence found in caves on Palawan indicates that about 50,000 years ago, an ancient people called the *Tabon* lived on the island. Eventually, other islands of the archipelago were settled by families arriving in boats called *barangay*, the name given to these settlements. The original settlements consisted of families that remained separated from each other over the many islands; as a result, different ways of speaking (languages and dialects) developed over thousands of years. About 87 languages and dialects are currently spoken in the Philippines. A national language called *Pilipino*, based on the central Luzon language *Tagalog*, was eventually established and is now taught and spoken in schools and businesses. Most Filipinos also continue to speak the language and dialect into which they were born.

About 3,000 years ago, when there were no longer any land bridges, people from other parts of Asia who were seeking trade found their way to the Philippine archipelago in long boats. Some settled on the islands and intermarried with the inhabitants.

About 1,100 years ago, around 900 A.D. or C.E. (C.E. means the common era), Arab traders came to the archipelago, primarily to the southern island, Mindanao. They brought with them their religion of Islam and spread it over many parts of the Philippines. Today, the Muslim religion is practiced by about 15% of Filipinos. Most of the Muslims live in Mindanao; they call themselves *Moros* and are agitating to be considered a separate country. This has led to armed conflict, ocket Stones **181**

now escalating, between the Moros and the Philippine government.

In the year 1519, about 480 years ago, a Portuguese navigator named Ferdinand Magellan became a citizen of Spain and, with ships and money supplied by the king of Spain, set out to find a westward route to the Spice Islands. It took him about one year to find a way from the Atlantic Ocean to the Pacific Ocean, passing through a strait in South America now called the Strait of Magellan. (You can find it on a map by looking near the southern tip of Argentina). In 1521, Magellan sighted the island of Samar in the Philippines and landed. He was welcomed by the friendly inhabitants, whom he subsequently converted to Catholicism. Several months later, while trying to convert the inhabitants of other islands to Catholicism, he was killed on the island of Mactan by warriors of the chief, Lapu-lapu, who did not want his people to be converted. The remaining Spaniards escaped back to Spain, including a historian named Pigafetta who recorded details of Magellan's voyage.

Subsequently, Spain supported several more voyages to the Philippines in order to capture the islands and include them in the Spanish empire. Ultimately, they succeeded because of their superior weapons and methods of warfare. The islands came under the domination of Spain in 1571 and were named in honor of the Spanish King Philip II.

Between the years 1600 and 1648, Dutch expeditions attempted to take over the Philippines from Spain but were not successful. In 1762, during the Seven Years War in Europe, the British captured Manila from Spain, but returned it in 1764, along with Cuba, at the Treaty of Paris. Thus, until the Spanish-American War in 1898, the Philippines was a colony of Spain for almost 400 years, and the Filipino people had very little freedom.

59-LEWI

A major goal of Spain, in addition to taking away as much of the island wealth as possible for the enrichment of Spain, was to convert all the people to Catholicism. They were so successful that, even today, more than 85% of the Filipinos are Catholics.

Along with Catholicism, Spain also brought Spanish-style culture and education to the Philippines, and many young Filipinos of wealthier families became priests, teachers, doctors, and lawyers. The vast majority of the people, however, received very little education, and they worked on rice, sugar cane, tobacco, and coconut plantations. Life under the rule of Spain for most Filipinos was hard and often cruel.

During the 1860s to 1880s, groups of young Filipinos went to Spain and other parts of Europe to continue their education. They were idealistic and seriously planned rebellion against Spanish rule. Prior to this, since the 1500s, there had been many sporadic uprisings by the Filipinos against the Spanish authorities, but all were defeated. It was also in the middle to late 1800s that Filipino newspapers began to publish. Although the Spanish authorities censored these newspapers, at least one openly advocated separation of the Philippines from Spain. In the 1870s, a series of executions, deportations, imprisonment, and flight of Filipino leaders led to a "reign of terror" imposed upon the people. In 1892, Dr. Jose Rizal, who had written two novels depicting the cruel life under Spanish rule (*Noli Me Tangere* and *El Filibusterismo*), returned to the Philippines from Europe. He established a society called *La Liga Filipina*, whose objectives were to defend all Filipinos against violence and injustice; to promote industry, agriculture, and business; and to study and apply reforms. Rizal was arrested soon after, deported, and executed in 1896. The day after Rizal's deportation, Andres Bonifacio and others organized an active revolutionary group known as the *katipunan*, and that same year they launched a full-scale revolution with armed attack of the Spanish *Guardia Civil* on the outskirts of Manila. Other revolutionary groups joined the *katipuneros*, but unfortunately, a power struggle sprang up within the revolutionary movement that ended with the arrest of Andres Bonifacio by corevolutionaries led by Emilio Aguinaldo. Bonifacio was tried for treason, found guilty, and executed in 1897. Aguinaldo continued the armed rebellion against Spain and called for guerrilla warfare all across Luzon. He was attempting to force Spain to agree to the rebels' demands: expulsion of the Spanish friars, assignment of the parishes equally between Spanish and Filipino priests, return of friar lands to previous Filipino owners, representation in the Spanish courts, freedom of press and religion, and equal rights for all persons. Eventually, a truce was declared, and terms of the truce were negotiated at *Biyak-na-Bato*. During the negotiation period, 50 revolutionary leaders met also at *Biyak-na-Bato* to establish the first constitutional government in the Philippines.

The truce pact was signed and included the surrender of rebel arms, exile of Aguinaldo and others to Hong Kong, and payment of money to the revolutionary leaders. Within a few months, however, both sides of the truce violated the pact, and the revolutionary war resumed.

About this same time, the United States was having trouble in Cuba, a country also in armed revolt against Spain. The American battleship "Maine" was blown up in Havana harbor, leading the United States to declare war against Spain. In April 1898, Undersecretary of War Theodore Roosevelt ordered Commodore George Dewey to capture or destroy the

Spanish fleet in Manila. On April 30, Dewey's fleet entered Manila Bay and destroyed every single Spanish ship.

The defeat of Spain by the United States raised the hopes of the Filipino revolutionary leaders that the U.S. Constitution would not allow colonization of the Philippines and that the Americans would help the Filipinos regain their independence from Spain. On May 19, Emilio Aguinaldo met with Commodore Dewey on board ship and left this meeting hopeful for the support of the United States in the Filipinos' struggle. Unknown to Aguinaldo, on this same day U.S. President McKinley ordered the occupation of the Philippines by the U.S. Armed Forces.

On June 12, 1898, Emilio Aguinaldo proclaimed independence for the Philippines in his hometown of Kawit in the province of Cavite and displayed his design for the Philippine flag. On June 18, with the help of Apolonario Mabini, a national congress was held in which Aguinaldo changed the form of government from dictatorial to constitutional.

On August 13, 1898, Spain formally surrendered to the United States. The next day General Merritt issued a proclamation stating " ... *we have not come to wage war upon them (the Filipinos) but to protect them ...* ," in effect declaring the occupation of the Philippines and its annexation as the first colony of the United States. President McKinley described the process as *"benevolent assimilation."*

On December 10, 1898, at the second Treaty of Paris, Spain ceded the Philippines to the United States for $20,000,000. During these negotiations, the Filipinos were treated as if they did not exist. The same treaty granted Cuba its independence and turned over Guam and Puerto Rico to the United States. McKinley ordered General Otis in Manila to post a proclamation to the effect that the Americans "*came, not as invaders or conquerors but as friends to protect the natives in their homes.* . . ." General Otis omitted the terms "*right of cession*" and "*immediate occupation*" from the version he posted. The Filipinos tore down the proclamations and trampled them. Thousands joined the revolutionary forces, and the Philippine-American war began. With far superior armaments, the American army (about 74,000 soldiers) defeated the Filipinos. Aguinaldo escaped and hid for two years, but he ultimately was captured in March 1901 and was presented to General Arthur MacArthur as a prisoner of war. He swore allegiance to the United States in April of that year.

You might ask why the American people allowed the annexation of the Philippines by the United States, when such an action violated all the principles that the American people held dear, as stated in their Constitution. One answer is that the American people and their representatives in Congress were kept unaware of the true situation by President McKinley. Another answer could be that the Filipino people were seen as ignorant natives who would be incapable of governing themselves. In any case, the Filipino people came under the governance of the United States for 40 years until World War II when the Japanese Army invaded the Philippines and conquered it in 1941.

Living conditions for Filipinos, particularly in cities and towns, improved markedly after some years under American rule. A Board of Health was established to combat the thousands of cases of tuberculosis, *beri-beri* (vitamin B deficiency), and other diseases such as bubonic plague. Sanitary systems were put into place that decreased epidemics of cholera, typhoid, and dysentery. Drinking water distribution systems were installed, and vaccination against smallpox was rigorously applied.

A public school system was established, initially staffed by Americans, but eventually taken over by Filipino teachers. The official language of instruction was English. In 1908, the University of the Philippines was opened so that Filipinos could attend college without going abroad.

The Filipinos lived under much more personal freedom than they had under Spain. Art, music, science, and other cultural activities were able to thrive, and the people were free to practice religions other than Catholicism. The right to vote for women was obtained in 1937 after great difficulty. But despite these improvements in general living conditions compared with conditions under the domination of Spain, the Filipinos were very much aware that they were still dominated by a foreign power. Pockets of armed resistance to the American presence continued, but they were no match for the superior weapons and organization of the American forces; captured rebels were often tortured.

The transfer of government from military to civil, and eventually to some measure of Filipino self-government, took place gradually. In 1916, U.S. President Woodrow Wilson signed the Philippine Autonomy Act (also known as the Jones Law) that established the American form of government in the Philippines, i.e., with judicial, legislative, and executive branches. The executive branch was placed under control of the American Governor General. The original Jones Bill in 1912 set the granting of independence to the Philippines eight years after passage of the law, but the bill was not passed by the U.S. Congress until the eight-year time frame was deleted. Manuel L. Quezon was elected first President of the Senate, and Sergio Osmena the first Speaker of the House of Representatives. In 1918, the Legislature created a commission to recommend ways to convince the U.S. government to grant Philippine independence. After several rejections and reorganization of various commissions to the United States, the Tydings-McDuffie Act, providing for Philippine independence after 10 years, was signed into law by President Franklin Roosevelt in March 1934. To prepare the Philippines for independence, a Commonwealth government with its own constitution, but taking its direction from the U.S. Congress, elected Manuel Quezon as the first President, and Sergio Osmena as the Vice president. To obtain U.S approval of the Philippine constitution, the framers included provisions sure to please the United States, such as equal civil rights for U.S. citizens in the Philippines and U.S. control over Philippine currency, coinage, trade, immigration, and foreign affairs. The Philippine constitution was approved in 1935.

Then, on December 7 and 8, 1941, the Japanese attacked the United States at Pearl Harbor in Hawaii and at Manila in the Philippines. By December 10, they had invaded northern Luzon. President Manuel Quezon, confined to a wheelchair with tuberculosis, escaped to Corregidor with his cabinet and with General Douglas MacArthur, who was then in command of the U.S. Armed Forces in the Far East. On February 20, Quezon and Osmena left the Philippines for Australia. MacArthur left on March 11, with the promise to return.

President Quezon died in Australia before MacArthur's return to the Philippines and subsequent defeat of the Japanese. Vice President Osmena returned to the Philippines with General MacArthur in October of 1944, landing in Leyte in the Visayan Islands. By the end of February 1945, the U.S. Armed Forces had liberated Manila. In August 1945, after the nuclear bombing of Hiroshima and Nagasaki, Japan surrendered to the United States. About a year later, on July 4, 1946, the United States granted independence to the Philippines. Manuel Roxas was sworn in as President and Elpidio Quirino as Vice President.

Since then, relations between the Philippines and the United States have generally been friendly—although at times rather thorny, particularly in regard to maintenance of U.S. Air Force and Navy bases in the Philippines. As the generation of Filipinos born after World War II has grown up, memories of the good and bad aspects under American governance have faded, and a new relationship has evolved.

The development of the Philippines as a nation has been bumpy. The growth rate of the population, currently 2.25%, is one of the highest in Southeast Asia. At this rate of growth, the population (now about 80 million) will double in 31 years. Economic growth has not kept up with population growth, due partly to the lack of energy resources such as oil, natural gas, or coal required for industrialization. This has led to a large proportion of poor people, a condition exacerbated by the continued concentration of wealth in a small minority (the oligarchy). Despoliation of natural resources for short-term gain, coupled with desires for a western-style standard of living, have rapidly deteriorated the environmental quality of the land that once was called the "Pearl of the Orient Seas." Internal armed conflict occurs due to economic desperation, for ideological reasons, or—in the case of the Moslem population on the island of Mindanao—a continuing struggle to become a separate country. Such conflict causes instability in the lives of the population in general, uses up precious government resources, and tends to discourage tourism. The lack of opportunities for job and intellectual advancement has led to the flight of many talented young people to foreign countries where their intelligence, education, and initiative are valued.

Despite this dismal scenario, the Filipino people maintain hope and pride in their nation and in their heritage. Unsung local scientists and government workers continue to study and alleviate environmental degradation, to increase food production, and to improve the health of families in rural areas. Well-meaning national leaders in both the public and private sectors of the country continue an uphill struggle to bring their country into a leadership position, both political and economic, among the nations of Southeast Asia. It is not always clear how these goals can be obtained in this period of economic "globalization", the effects of which are not easily controlled or predicted. Underlying this struggle is a fierce spirit of independence that brings to mind a statement attributed to Manuel L. Quezon: "I would rather see the Philippines run like hell by the Filipinos, than like heaven by the Americans."

Bibliographic sources for this historical summary:

Corpus, O.D. 1989. *The Roots of the Filipino Nation.* Aklahi Foundation, Inc.

National Centennial Commission, 1999. *100 Events That Shaped the Philippines.*

Steinberg, R. 1979. *Return to the Philippines.* Time-Life Books, Inc.

Population Reference Bureau. 2000 World Population Data Sheet. http://www.prb.org/pubs/wpds2000.